ABSTRACT EXPRESSIONISM

BARRON'S
Woodbury, New York

For Richard

First U.S. Edition 1978
Barron's Educational Series, Inc.

Text filmset by Keyspools Ltd, Golborne, Lancs
Litho origination by Paramount Litho Ltd, Wickford, Essex
Printed in Great Britain by Cox and Wyman Ltd,
London, Fakenham and Reading

Library of Congress Catalog Card No. 77-80188
International Standard Book No. 0-8120-0880-4

Printed in Great Britain

ABSTRACT EXPRESSIONISM

The social and political upheavals of the Depression and the disruption caused by the war against Hitler had a profound effect on young artists in Europe and America. Technological advances no longer seemed a guarantee of social or political progress. The hopeful rationalism of modern society was discredited. As far as art was concerned, the logical, idealistic premises of Cubism and the movements which flowed from it in the years between the two wars had lost their appeal.

The generation which began to paint in the 1930s and early 1940s was in a desperate frame of mind. A new approach was urgently needed to resolve what was seen as a crisis of subject matter. 'The situation was so bad that I know I felt free to try anything, no matter how absurd it seemed,' the American painter Adolph Gottlieb observed. He and many of his contemporaries were tentatively moving towards an aesthetic which repudiated the hegemony of intellect and allowed the artist to express himself freely and subjectively. As another American, Robert Motherwell, put it: 'The need is for felt experience – intense, immediate, direct, subtle, unified, warm, vivid, rhythmic.'

Many painters began to concentrate on the act of painting itself, unimpeded by anything save the decision to paint. Their thinking rested on an already well-established principle. If they emptied their minds of preconceptions, and applied pigment with a maximum of spontaneity, the images they made would be an expression of the deepest levels of their being. Everybody was agreed that this was a worthy objective: modern depth psychology appeared to show that the conscious mind could exert a repressive authority on the unconscious, and that, if it released its hold, the springs of feeling would flow clear again. Art, then, became a method of self-realization.

The Surrealists had shown the way. Taking their cue from the procedures of psychoanalysis – especially free association – they formulated the technique of automatism, according to which the painter or writer operated, metaphorically speaking, blindfold. He welcomed accident and exploited the random, doing anything in fact that would send the ego to sleep. André Breton's original definition of Surrealism in 1924 still held good: 'Pure psychic automatism by which it is intended to express, either verbally or in writing [he soon enlarged this to include visual art], the true function of thought. Thought dictated in the absence of all control exerted by reason, and outside all aesthetic or moral preoccupations.'

Other influences were at work as well. Many artists were indebted to Paul Klee, who took a post-Freudian interest in dreams and combined a sophisticated wit with child-like candour. In fact, the simplicities of the art of children and psychotics were felt by many to be as instructive as the work of their own professional antecedents. A group of Northern European artists drew German Expressionism into a vigorous, painterly style. The so-called matter painters devised a novel variant of collage: by mixing sand, plaster and other materials with pigment they gave the flat canvas something of the three-dimensional solidity of sculpture.

It was not only a re-evaluation of the contemporary Western tradition that contributed to the new emphasis on gesture or 'the act of painting'. Artists found much in Oriental art, and more particularly calligraphy, which threw light on their crisis of

4

subject matter. In Chinese calligraphy, the brush-stroke is of prime importance. The painter-scribe abolishes the contradiction between subject and object, and, by concentrating on the process of sign-making, feels that he is actively participating in a continuous and potentially endless series of events (paralleling the cosmic process of generation and regeneration). In a telling phrase, a Chinese commentator, Père Tchang-Ming, remarked that ideograms are 'congealed gestures'.

Perhaps it is worth drawing a connection between graffiti in public places and calligraphy: graffiti too are congealed gestures, and the fact that these gestures represent, not a sense of unity with all things as in Oriental art, but a social estrangement, appealed to disillusioned men for whom painting was a heroic assertion of their identity. Far from escaping from self in the Eastern manner, they wished to proclaim it. Creativity was a sequence of free, unconditioned choices, through which they could redeem their alienation from society and from the given aesthetic tradition. It was a form of self-defence.

Existentialism offered a theoretical basis for this attitude, perhaps more as a climate of opinion than as a coherent philosophy. The writings of Jean-Paul Sartre provide the classic texts; and abstract artists, both in America and Europe, sympathized with his argument that man alone is responsible for his fate, which he has to make and re-make for himself. Man's consciousness is subjective and can never become aware of itself objectively and surely except through the 'gaze of the Other'. If other people function as mirrors in which to see oneself, so too can the work of art. Sartre did not hold a 'salvation through art' position for long, but it is a concept which had an interesting resonance for the many artists who found themselves in an isolated situation. It enabled them to acquire self-assurance by means of their work; and the Existentialist thesis that 'being is doing' gave intellectual justification to an approach which emphasized *process* at the expense of *product*.

Within this whole tradition of 'the act of painting', there is a radical distinction to be drawn between the School of Paris and the New York School. Painters in France never really abandoned content as ordinarily defined – a message or a sign – and even the traditional principles of composition can be detected in their work. New York painters tried hard to go beyond both. They explored the full implications of the discovery that 'what was to go on the canvas was not a picture but an event'.

New York Background

The American artist has always been a loner, and he was one of the first to suffer from the economic débâcle of the 1920s and 1930s. Patrons were few and far between, and, when they did buy his work, treated him as a courtier paid to cater to their tastes. The general public had little time for him, and his status was to be neatly illustrated during the Second World War by the lists of those without a right to deferment of military service: 'clerks, messengers, office-boys, shipping clerks, watchmen, footmen, bellboys, pages, sales clerks, filing clerks, hair dressers, dress and millinery makers, designers, interior decorators and artists'.

Nevertheless, something had to be done to support professional painters and sculptors during the Depression if they were not to be forced on to the streets. A few experimented, more or less unsuccessfully, with self-help schemes; and a group of New Yorkers picked up an idea from France for avoiding dealers and bartering direct with the public: work would be exchanged for 'anything reasonable'.

Rescue came from the unlikely direction of the Federal Government. In December 1933, as Roosevelt's New Deal got under way, the Public Works of

Art Project was set up. In the half-year of its existence it hired 3,749 artists who turned out 15,633 works of art for public institutions. This was doing pretty well, but not well enough. The more ambitious Federal Art Project, which came to be known as the 'Project', took the principles of the PWAP a stage further. Within twelve months over 5,500 artists, teachers, craftsmen, photographers, designers and researchers were in the Project's employ. The salary was $95 a month for 96 hours' work. Easel painters were expected to submit periodic evidence of studio activity.

The politicians were probably hoping that culture would in this way be harnessed to the country's new-found social idealism. 'Could we, through actors and artists who had themselves known privation, carry music and plays to children in city parks, and art galleries to little towns?' asked Harry Hopkins, to whom Roosevelt had entrusted responsibility for the various art relief programmes. 'Were not happy people at work the greatest bulwark of democracy?'

This optimism did not in the event do much to alter the ingrained American suspicion of the arts. Free concerts in hospitals or schools, and murals in post offices, were of greater aid to the producer than to the consumer. For the Project's historic achievement was to bring artists together and give them a chance to pursue their interests freely and with a minimum of economic distraction. Thus, Willem De Kooning was able to take up painting full time only when he landed a contract with the Project.

The American art scene at the time was fragmented. Representational painters rallied to the flag, and under the general heading of Regionalism offered a folksy celebration of the American agrarian past – perhaps in compensation for the collapse of industry. With the rise of Fascism many younger talents became pre-occupied with international socialism. In New York the Communist Party attracted artists of many aesthetic persuasions, including a devoted band of Social Realists. Their canvases are radical and polemical, and deal with issues such as the gaoling of a leading trade unionist and the Sacco and Vanzetti affair. A dynamic realism indebted to the Mexican revolutionary painters José Clemente Orozco, David Alfaro Siqueiros and Diego Rivera, was the order of the day.

Both the Regionalists and the Social Realists turned their back on abstraction and the inventions of the European avant-garde. However, since the epoch-making Armory Show of 1913, a faltering abstract tradition had come into being. Josef Albers founded an association of painters in 1937 called American Abstract Artists. It staged exhibitions, published books and organized lectures. Its members decisively rejected Impressionism, Expressionism, and above all Surrealism, for a structural, geometric, post-Cubist manner. But young painters soon tired of AAA's derivative formulas. The innovators of Abstract Expressionism stayed away, preferring to meet in loose groupings of their own.

Regionalism and Social Realism ran out of steam too; both styles were too restricted to allow for much experiment or change. Artists discovered that left-wing politics were time-consuming, and that they had their knuckles rapped if they stepped out of line. The painter Stuart Davis, an ardent activist, broke his friendship with Arshile Gorky for this reason: 'I took the business as seriously as the serious situation demanded and devoted much time to the organizational work. Gorky was less intense about it and still wanted to play.'

Naturally, those for whom the business of painting was more than 'play' fell away. Others were shaken by the Nazi-Soviet non-aggression pact of 1939, and support for the Communists declined.

The Second World War led to the arrival in the United States of many key figures of twentieth-century art, in exile from their home countries – Breton, Chagall, Ernst, Léger, Lipchitz, Masson, Matta and Mondrian among them. Surrealists such as Masson and Matta, who offered spontaneous, semi-abstract canvases filled with forms drawn from the depths of the unconscious, were now a direct presence, not a remote example. By chance of war New York assumed the mantle of Paris; Americans felt at the centre of affairs for the first time and no longer in a cultural outback. The effect of this can hardly be exaggerated.

In 1943 the Federation of Modern Painters and Sculptors pointed to the parallel between America's new international political role and her increasing strength in the arts: 'As a nation we are now being forced to outgrow our narrow political isolationism. Now that America is recognized as the centre where art and artists of the world meet, it is time for us to accept cultural values on a truly global plane.'

If there is a single quality which distinguishes the American Abstract Expressionists from their contemporaries elsewhere, it is an intensity of purpose which allowed them to ride roughshod over both stylistic convention and what Clement Greenberg called 'paint quality'. Greenberg argued that the American vision was characterized by a 'fresher, opener, more immediate surface', offensive to standard taste. He related this quality to a 'more intimate and habitual acquaintance with isolation', which was, in his view, 'the condition under which the true quality of the age is experienced'.

Myths and Symbols

André Breton, the chief ideologue of Surrealism, wrote in 1927: 'Freud has shown that there prevails in the "unfathomable" depths a total absence of contradiction, a new mobility of the emotional blocks caused by repression, a timelessness and a substitution of psychic reality for external reality, all subject to the principle of pleasure alone. Automatism leads straight to this region.'

However, neither psychic reality nor pleasure principle were enough in themselves; and instead of Sigmund Freud the New York painters looked to C. G. Jung, for whom the unconscious opened doors not merely to individual neuroses but to the universal archetypes of human experience. His view was that the unconscious is 'mythopoetic' – that it naturally creates myths – and that the arts are an important means by which myths and symbols are kept alive in an otherwise one-sidedly 'conscious' world.

Jung showed that primitive art was a virgin quarry of symbols that were as relevant to the contemporary world as they had been in the prehistoric past. Mark Rothko observed in 1943: 'Those who think that the world is more gentle and graceful than the primeval and predatory passions from which these myths sprang are either not aware of reality or do not wish to see it in art. The myth . . . expresses to us something real and existing in ourselves, as it was to those who first stumbled upon the symbols to give them life.'

The young Jackson Pollock was interested in Jung as early as the mid-1930s, and went to a Jungian analyst when he began psychiatric treatment for alcoholism in 1937. He equated what he saw as the best contemporary Western art with American Indian painting, praising the Indians for their 'capacity to get hold of appropriate images and their understanding of what constitutes painterly subject matter'.

9,15 The imagery that Pollock and his fellows employed was based on 'biomorphic' forms related to animal and plant structures, to primitive symbols, to the shapes that flow from a free handling of paint, and to the semi-conscious patterns of automatism.

Arshile Gorky stands rather to one side of the new mythic manner; his 'hybrids' (to use Breton's expression) are related to it in character, but they also have the obsessive sexuality of a Freud-based Surrealism. He did not cut his bridges to Europe, and should perhaps be regarded as a precursor of the New York School who happened to overlap its first decade, rather than a founder member. Born Vosdanig Manoog Adoian in Turkish Armenia in 1904, he arrived in the United States from Eastern Europe in 1920. He studied at the Rhode Island School of Design and later the Grand Central School of Art, where he was both pupil and teacher. He acquired a reputation as a brilliant *pasticheur*, and his early work bears witness to an almost programmatic intention to live through most of the major styles of modern art.

His starting point was Impressionism, but he soon graduated to Cézanne and to Synthetic Cubism. Between 1929 and 1934 Picasso, Braque and Gris
2 were major influences (as in the *Composition* of 1932–33), and he was nicknamed 'the Picasso of Washington Square'. 'I was *with* Cézanne for a long time,' he remarked, 'and now naturally I am with Picasso.' Gorky then moved on to Tanguy, Masson and Matta (for their unstable shifting spaces) and Mirò (for his curlicued figures). Around 1936 he adopted a biomorphic abstract style. In the early 1940s he became interested in Kandinsky.

Gorky was not unaware of the dangers of his situation. According to a possibly apocryphal anecdote, he called some fellow-artists to his studio in the mid-1930s and told them sadly: 'Let's face it, we're bankrupt.' Whatever the truth of the matter, a proud tactfulness or a dilettante sensibility delayed Gorky's artistic maturity until the final years of his short life; he killed himself following a cancer operation in 1946 and a car crash in which he broke his neck.

Around 1943, in his *Garden in Sochi* series, he made
1 his breakthrough. In *Water of the Flowery Mill* the paint lies in thin, brilliant washes of colour which are allowed to overflow and overlap. Soft, feminine

forms mingle with spiky masculine ones, and although they refer to Gorky's aesthetic forebears (the Synthetic Cubists in this instance) they are distinguished by a dreamy, meandering feeling for line. His encounter with the Surrealists in New York had given him the confidence to experiment with spontaneous draughtsmanship which submerged, if it did not eliminate, his Cubist inheritance.

Gorky's hybrids, curious vegetable and animal composites, suggest a mental doodling in front of nature. In his eyes landscape had a symbolic and sexual content, which stems from memories of his childhood in rural Armenia. Had he lived, it is hard to resist the impression that his playful epicureanism would have set him apart from the other Abstract Expressionists; his work lacks the urgency of Pollock or Newman.

3 Thus, in *The Betrothal II*, painted in 1947, pale greenish-yellow figures outlined in black stand against warm ochre; bristly verticals mingle with visceral fruit-like forms. The canvas retains the freshness of a sketch while also attaining a kind of academic classicism: not for nothing was Gorky called 'the Ingres of the unconscious', and behind some of his rounded shapes lies the example of Ingres' *Odalisques*.

William Baziotes' work came into sharp focus during this 'mythic' phase of Abstract Expressionism, and did not change radically thereafter. He agreed with Jung's emphasis on 'a primordial art', which allows 'a glimpse into the unfathomed abyss of what has not yet become'. This 'abyss' often resembles an undersea world where protozoic marine forms float in a filtered light. Amoebic dwarfs, spiders and birds are also included in Baziotes' scheme of things. 'Every one of us finds water either a symbol of peace or fear,' he wrote in 1948. 'I know I never feel better than when I gaze for a long time at the bottom of a still pond.' But the silence and order of his pictures is not usually placid, and the symbols which people them are discrete, sinister and obsessive.

Born in 1912, Baziotes came to New York from Pittsburgh in 1933, studied at the National Academy of Design, and joined the Federal Art Project. He worked in comparative obscurity before showing at Peggy Guggenheim's Art of This Century Gallery in 1944. He was influenced by the precise, exotic colours of Persian miniatures and also by Klee, Mirò and, especially, Picasso. In 1940 he met the Surrealist Matta and was excited by the idea that abstraction could be a vehicle for psychic meanings. In 1942 he was represented in the New York 'International Surrealist Exhibition'.

Baziotes learned to equalize the surface tension of his designs by eliminating sculptural or three-dimensional depth and replacing it with an integrated paint surface and an all-over tonal harmony. Also, with time, he reduced the number and increased the
23 size of his figures. *Dwarf*, painted in 1947, shows Baziotes at the height of his powers. The fuzzy green figure and the mauve ground are tonally similar, and the all-over effect is reinforced by his method of painting – a soft brushing which gives the picture surface a mistily liquid quality. From 1950 until his death in 1963 Baziotes moved in the direction of greater sophistication and control. His later works have a tasteful decorativeness which is matched by a certain caution and avoidance of risk.

The All-over Field

It is not surprising that the American artists, interested as they were in the processes of painting and drawing, should have responded with enthusiasm to some aspects of Oriental art, in particular Chinese calligraphy. Mark Tobey was one of the first to pay serious attention to East Asian painting, although he was not personally associated with the New York

School. Like his Oriental masters, he pursued a calmly meditative goal. Born in Wisconsin in 1890, he taught in Seattle on the West Coast between 1922 and 1925. During this period he became interested in American Indian art and Japanese woodcuts. A convert to the Baha'i World Faith, a universalistic and optimistic religious sect, he devoted himself to the reconciliation and union of Eastern and Western cultures. He studied Eastern painting at the University of Washington, taught at Dartington Hall in England, and in 1934 travelled to China and Japan where he spent a month in a Zen monastery.

This journey liberated his aesthetic development, and on his return he started the series of paintings called 'white writings' which continued through the
14 1940s and 1950s. In *Edge of August*, painted in 1953, we see the culmination of Tobey's adaptation of calligraphy to painting. A labyrinth of white thread-like script lies on a reddish ground: perspective is destroyed, and form, to use his own words, 'smashed'. The communicative function of the sign gives way to a rhythmic working which creates an all-over texture and effectively dematerializes the brush-stroke. The best of Tobey has a slight fussy tranquillity; because his central area of concern is religious, he never identified himself with the Abstract Expressionists' drastic re-evaluation of the bases of contemporary art.

Tobey's 'white writings' resemble Jackson Pollock's 'drip paintings'. The comparison comes out to Pollock's credit, and once again the issue resolves itself into one of intensity. Pollock was prepared to 'go the full length'. As in the case of Rimbaud, this entailed a profligacy of effort, a capacity to push his luck to the point of incoherence in his work, and perhaps of self-destruction in his life. More than any of his contemporaries he dared to test his ideas till the cracks showed and they began to give way. This authenticity, or, in Sartre's phrase, 'good faith', has been as influential as his pictures.

To trace his career is to analyse the key elements in the gestural phase of the New York School; and, although he did not make all the technical discoveries (Hans Hofmann, for instance, was the first to use a drip technique), he can lay claim to their most energetic exploitation. Born in 1912 on a sheep ranch in Wyoming, Pollock was the son of relatively poor parents ('excellent craftsmen', according to his brother Charles, 'they knew how to grow things, they knew how to make things. But neither of them had a sense for business or commercial profit'). The family moved house many times during his childhood. There was little in his background to suggest he would become an artist.

His rise to fame is in the classic mould of the American success story: from the Wild West he travelled to the big city, took the world by storm, but found his triumph hard to manage. The prototype for this kind of folk hero is the early twentieth-century author Jack London; and the lives of the two men have a number of curious analogies. Like London, Pollock had a severe drink problem and died at the height of his celebrity, exhausted and apparently in despair. Some critics have suggested that the geography of the West and the ceaseless travels of his early years left their mark on Pollock's painting. He certainly enjoyed the immensity of the American landscape and the temptations of the open road; it may be no accident that it was on the open road he died, in 1956, violently driving his car too fast round a bend and crashing into a tree.

D.H. Lawrence, in an essay on Walt Whitman, offers some insights into American culture which are remarkably apposite to Pollock and to his fellow-frontiersmen of the New York School: 'It is the American heroic message. The soul is not to pile up defences round herself. She is not to withdraw and seek her heavens inwardly, in mystical ecstasies. She is not to cry to some God beyond, for salvation. She is to go down the open road, as the road opens, into the unknown, keeping company with those whose soul draws them near to her, accomplishing nothing save the journey, and the works incidental to the journey.'

It took some time before the young Pollock came into direct contact with the international avant-garde. By 1930 he and his brother were studying painting under Thomas Benton at the Art Students' League. Benton was a Romantic Regionalist of a reactionary turn of mind: 'I wallowed in every cockeyed ism that came along and it took me ten years to get all the modernist dirt out of my system,' he is reported to have said. He had made his name with vigorously distorted and sometimes satirical accounts of the American scene.

Pollock reacted *through* Benton rather than against him, abandoning his realistic subject matter but picking on and developing the older man's feeling for painterly rhythms which he in turn had drawn from Rubens, Michelangelo and El Greco. In *The*
9 *Flame*, painted in 1937, there is a recognizable content, but it is subordinated to Pollock's fascination with pigment, tonal contrasts and a heightened tempestuousness of treatment.

In 1935 Pollock worked for the Federal Art Project; he admired the Mexican revolutionary artists and took note of Kandinsky, Mirò, Klee, and the Surrealists, including Masson. But the strongest influence of all was Picasso. Pollock spent nearly ten years developing a semi-figurative symbolic vocabulary. His interest in Jung has already been remarked on, and he paid cautious tribute to the Surrealists. His pictures illustrate, in a partly automatist style, primitive myths, especially those which dealt with passionate sexuality. Three characteristic titles from 1943 were *Pasiphaë* (which was to have been called *Moby Dick*), *The She-Wolf* and *The Moon Woman Cuts the Circle*.

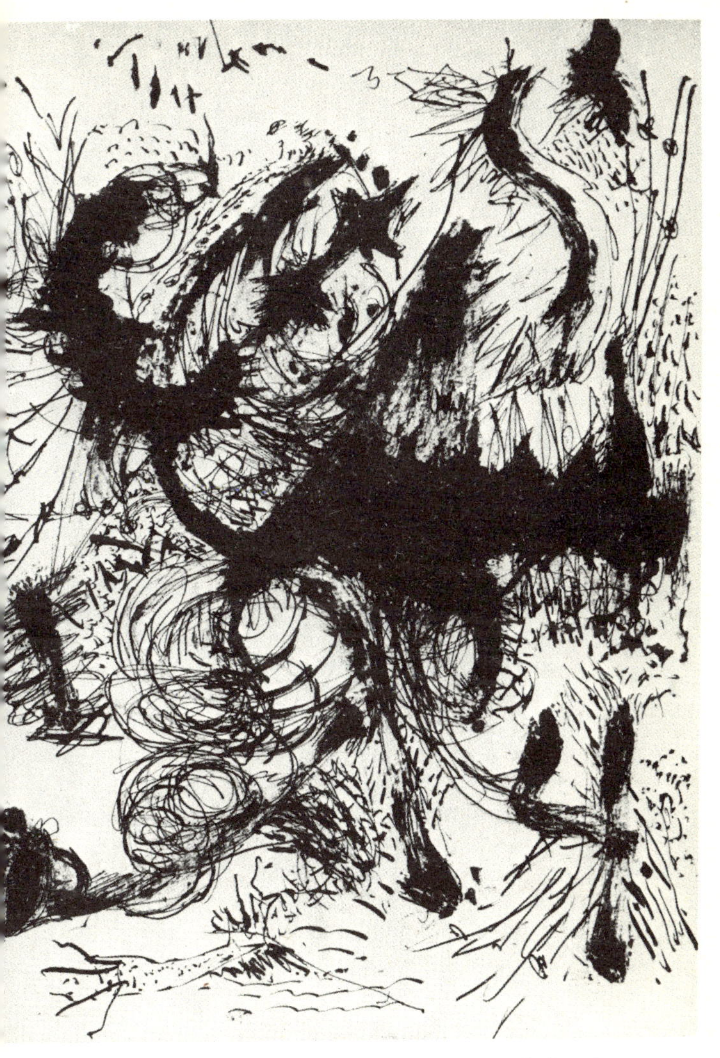

Jackson Pollock. *Drawing, c.* 1948. Black ink on paper, $11\frac{1}{4} \times 8$ (28.6×20.3). Lee Krasner Pollock, New York.

8 *The She-Wolf* illustrates Pollock's preoccupation with totem motifs. However, the violent composition and crudely vigorous brushwork also embody private anxieties. The wolf's red, unwinking eye falls in line with the disembodied eyes which recur cryptically throughout Pollock's career.

In 1947 recognizable imagery disappeared, and his canvases became surfaces which simply recorded his passage. The conventional techniques and materials of painting were not flexible or sensitive enough for this purpose; so Pollock devised his famous 'drip' method of applying paint. This is how he described it:

'My painting does not come from the easel. I hardly ever stretch my canvas before painting. I prefer to tack the unstretched canvas to the hard wall or the floor. I need the resistance of a hard surface. On the floor I am more at ease. I feel nearer, more a part of the painting, since this way I can walk around it, work from the four sides and literally be *in* the painting. This is akin to the method of the Indian sand painters of the West.

'I continue to get further away from the usual painter's tools such as easel, palette, brushes, etc. I prefer sticks, trowels, knives, and dripping fluid paint or a heavy impasto with sand, broken glass and other foreign matter added.'

12 Three masterpieces, *Cathedral* painted in 1947,
11,10 *One (No. 31)*, painted in 1950, and *Blue Poles*, painted in 1953, reveal the extent of Pollock's originality. His previously glutinous pigmentation yields to an airy grace. A shallow space is created, but does not subvert the substantiality of the materials used nor the integrity of the picture plane. The composition is an all-over field; despite the fact that the network of threads and cords of paint is usually contained within the edges of the canvas, it could, the spectator senses, be indefinitely extended. This is reinforced by the size of Pollock's paintings: they resemble portable

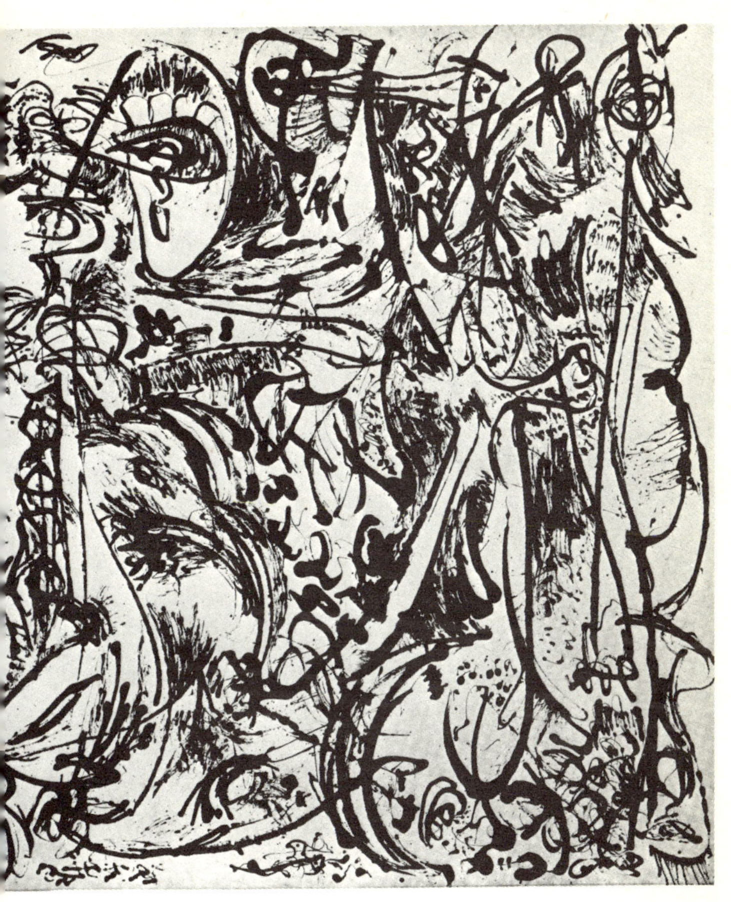

Jackson Pollock. *Echo,* 1951. Oil on canvas, $91\frac{7}{8} \times 86$ (233.4×218.4). The Museum of Modern Art, New York. Acquired through the Lillie P. Bliss Bequest and the Mr and Mrs David Rockefeller Fund.

murals and establish the New York School's preoccupation with scale: 'There was a reviewer a while back who wrote that my pictures didn't have any beginning or any end. He didn't mean it as a compliment, but it was. It was a fine compliment.'

The predominance of black and white in *Cathedral* is a reminder that Pollock is essentially a draughtsman. The critic Frank O'Hara noted his 'amazing ability to quicken a line by thinning it, to slow it by flooding, to elaborate that simplest of elements, the line – to change, to re-invigorate, to extend, to build up an embarrassment of riches in the mass of drawing alone'.

Above all, in these pictures, there is an overpowering release of energy, a euphoric dynamism. Pollock used to work very rapidly, after slow periods of walking around the canvas and brooding. What looks like chance is at most the exploitation of chance: 'When I am painting, I have a general notion as to what I am about. I *can* control the flow of paint: there is no accident.' At the same time, decisions were passive rather than active (as one would expect of an inheritor of Surrealist automatism): 'I have no fears about making changes, destroying the image, etc., because the painting has a life of its own. I try to let it come through.'

By 1953 Pollock found that he had exhausted the potential of 'drip' painting. His personal life was also in confusion, and, after two teetotal years, he withdrew again into alcoholism. He abandoned colour and returned to figuration. One consequence was the loss of the field effect, and his designs break down into broad puddled areas of pigment. He produced
13 many fine things, many of which – *Easter and the Totem*, painted in 1953, is a case in point – denote a return to his old subject matter with more sophisticated means.

Pollock's contemporaries in New York watched his career with mounting excitement, for it raised in an undiluted form many of the aesthetic preoccupations of the day. More than anything else, it represented a commitment to emotional honesty. Robert Motherwell wrote in 1950: 'The process of painting then is conceived of as an adventure, without preconceived ideas, on the part of persons of intelligence, sensibility and passion. Fidelity to what occurs between oneself and the canvas, no matter how unexpected, becomes central. . . . The major decisions in the process of painting are on the grounds of truth, not taste. . . . No artist ends up with the style he expected to have when he began.'

Willem De Kooning shared the leadership of the New York gestural avant-garde with Pollock. However, he remained on far closer terms with his aesthetic antecedents than did many of his peers. The movement which specially attracted him was Cubism; but his general attachment to tradition can also be seen in his acceptance of the human figure as a suitable subject for painting.

Born in Rotterdam in 1904, he spent his first twenty-one years in Europe and studied in Antwerp, Brussels and Rotterdam. He moved to the United States in 1926, but only started to paint full-time when he found employment with the Federal Arts Project. In his early work he painfully came to grips with the problem of treating three-dimensional figures without upsetting the integrity of the picture surface. In works of the early to middle 1940s, from the
5,4 *Seated Woman* of 1940 to the *Pink Angel* of 1947, his
solution was to play down modelling and, gradually, to isolate individual parts of the human body and treat them as planes. Painterly silhouettes, suggesting household objects and also biomorphic forms (he was a close friend of Arshile Gorky), are crowded together on a plain ground; there is little sense of space, of *in front* or *behind*, and the images and the gaps between them become to some extent interchangeable.

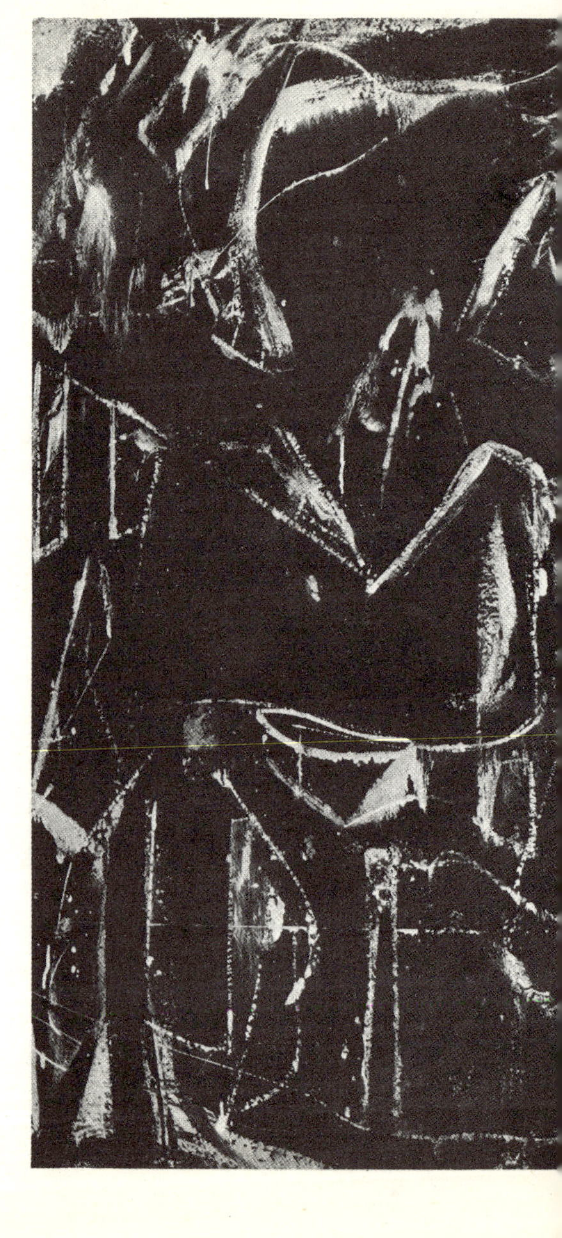

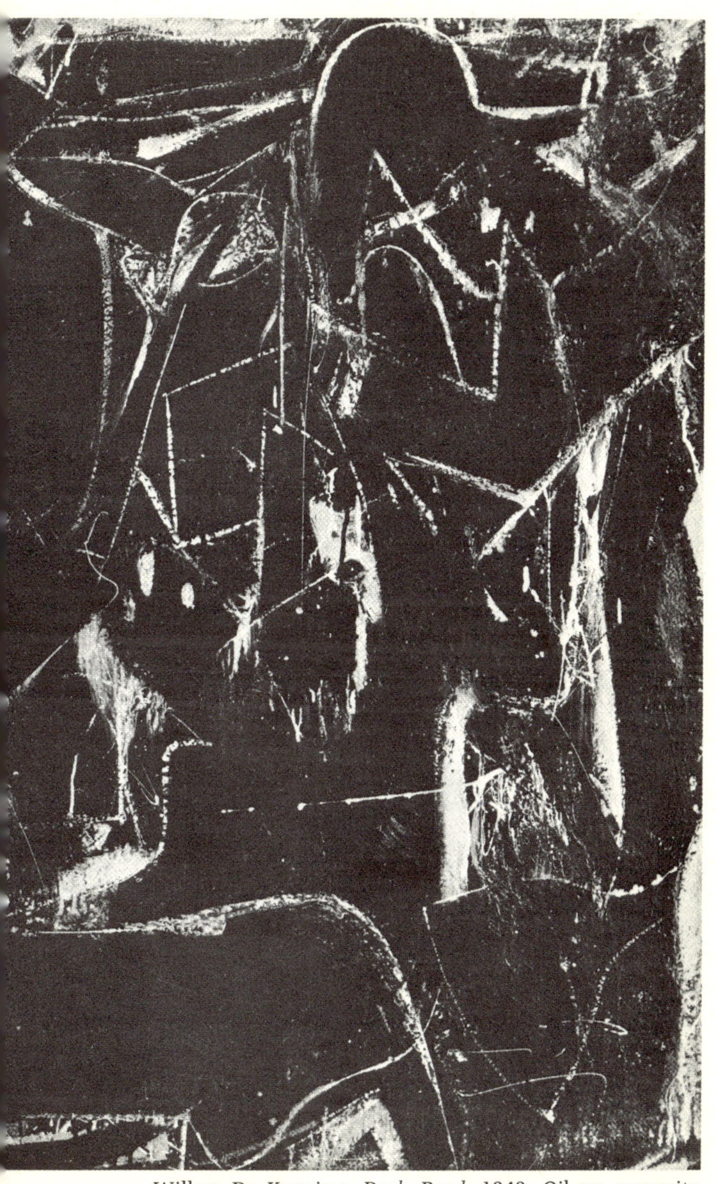

Willem De Kooning. *Dark Pond,* 1948. Oil on masonite, 46½ × 55½ (118.1 × 141). Collection Mr and Mrs Richard L. Weisman, New York.

After 1942, De Kooning experimented with automatism, which loosened his handling of paint and encouraged him to exploit the ambiguity of semi-abstract signs. It also introduced a new vehemence into his brushwork. All this laid the ground for his sudden adoption in 1947 of a new style in a series of black and white pictures in household enamel paint (he was too poor at the time to afford oils). Individual anatomical segments are now released from their representational context and are assembled, in (say) *Dark Pond*, painted in 1948, as a fleshy jigsaw – what one critic called a 'wall of living musculature'. There is now no distinction at all between figure and field. De Kooning painted a succession of remarkable pictures in a similar vein, at the same time returning to
6 colour: an example is the *Excavation* of 1950.

De Kooning was not a gesture-for-gesture's-sake artist who happened to retain an element of figuration; the significance of his subject matter was seldom far from his mind. 'Art never seems to make me peaceful or pure,' he said in 1951. 'I always seem to be wrapped in the melodrama of vulgarity.' Seldom making concessions to economic necessity, and living the Bohemian life of a 'loft rat', he expressed his own restless response to the modern city.

Around 1951, he resumed his *Women*, monstrously ugly but seductive females – part fertility goddesses, part graffiti. It was an obsessive image: 'It did one thing for me: it eliminated composition, arrangement, relationships, light – all this silly talk about line, colour and form – because that [i.e. the *Women*] was the thing I wanted to get hold of.'

In 1955 De Kooning returned to semi-abstraction, this time recalling 'landscapes and highways and sensations of that, outside the city – the feeling of going to the city or coming from it'. He simplified his draughtsmanship and enlivened his palette. In
7 *Door to the River*, painted in 1960, there is a broad, expansive painterliness – almost as if the artist had

reworked a blown-up detail of an earlier composition. In the 1960s he resumed the *Women* theme – but now his figures are softer, more fluid and palpable.

Because De Kooning had little to offer the colour field artists of the 1960s he has been neglected to the advantage of Pollock. His great achievements lie in combining a personal content with a repudiation of style (in the sense of stylishness), and in marrying figuration to an extreme gestural manner.

Pollock and, to a lesser extent, De Kooning turned their canvases into all-over fields by means of a lattice of brushmarks or drips; but other artists, among them Mark Rothko, Clyfford Still and Barnett Newman, were more interested in colour than gesture. Flat areas of paint replaced impasto and line. 'Instead of using outlines, instead of making shapes or setting off spaces, my drawings declare the space,' Newman wrote; 'instead of working with the remnants of space, I work with the whole space.'

Scale was a major ingredient. As Clement Greenberg put it in 1948, 'There is a persistent urge, as persistent as it is largely unconscious, to go beyond the cabinet picture, which is designed to occupy only a spot on the wall, to a kind of picture that, without actually becoming identified with the wall, like a mural, would spread over it and acknowledge its physical reality.'

Very large canvases altered the relation of the spectator to the work: he was no longer able to 'take it in' or frame it with a single glance. In fact, he was often overtaken by an expanse of colour which stretched beyond his range of vision. Rothko argued in 1951 that 'To paint a small picture is to place yourself outside your experience, to look upon an experience as a stereopticon view or with a reducing glass. However you paint the larger picture, you are in it. It isn't something you command.' It was now no longer an object in an environment but an environment in itself.

Objects of great size are awe-inspiring, and the fact that colour field pictures were not only very large in themselves but, like some of Pollock's work, contained implications of boundlessness, suited the transcendental aspirations of Newman and Rothko. They used the all-over colour field as an assertion of the mystery of being. Newman is fond of the term 'sublime', and refers to Edmund Burke's *Philosophical Enquiry into the Origin of Our Ideas of the Sublime and the Beautiful* for a definition. According to Burke's elaboration of the classical author Longinus, the basis of beauty is pleasure, and that of sublimity is pain or fear. Space, solitude, vastness and infinity (among other things) lead to the sublime. Newman's 'non-relational' canvases, empty of everything but colour and (as he says) drained of 'the impediments of memory, association, nostalgia, legend, myth or what have you', fitted the bill. The New York painters were not scholars; they picked on Burke because his ideas lent the authority of tradition to their style of painting, a style which, in Motherwell's words: 'becomes sublime when the artist transcends his personal anguish, when he projects in the midst of a shrieking world an expression of living and its end that is silent and ordered'.

Barnett Newman was born in New York in 1905 and died there in 1970; he studied at the Art Students' League, City College of New York and Cornell University. He taught during the 1930s, and did not participate in the Federal Arts Project: 'I paid a severe price for not being on the project with the other guys; in their eyes I wasn't a painter; I didn't have a label.' During the 1930s he was attracted by left-wing thinking, and he has been quoted as saying: 'My politics went towards open forms and free situations; I was a very vocal anarchist.'

Newman was an important polemicist, and passed through all the phases of Abstract Expressionism. In 1947, with Rothko, Motherwell and Baziotes, he helped to found a school called 'Subjects of the Artist' and to edit *Tiger's Eye*, a magazine which argued the case for an aesthetic based on myth. Although he rebelled against academic Surrealism, Newman explored automatist procedures. The archetypal forms and plastic energy of the North-West Coast Indians impressed him, as did pre-Columbian art; 'My idea was that, with an automatic move, you could create a world.'

31 Something of what he meant appears in *Untitled*
(1945); the gesture creates a world in which biomorphs and a prophetic road-like band cross a remote, creamy cosmic space. By 1948 Newman was ready to abandon subject matter, whether abstract or figura-
32 tive. *Onement I*, painted in that year, marks the
turning point in his style. A thickly painted vertical strip lies just off-centre over masking tape. No doubt Newman had intended quite another picture; and, as Charles Harrison points out, the refusal to lift the tape or to 'paint up' the ground were major and long-meditated decisions.

The picture prefigures the basic features of his later work. A repudiation of sensuously handled paint goes hand in hand with the disappearance of 'form' – that is, of pictorial elements and of design. The canvas becomes an undifferentiated field which is defined rather than divided by the stripe (or, as in *Vir*
33 *Heroicus Sublimis*, painted in 1950–51, stripes). These
thin bands neutrally echo the boundaries of the picture plane, and read like a serial sequence which could be repeated indefinitely beyond them.

But for all its importance, drawing is subordinate
34 to colour. In *Vir Heroicus Sublimis* and in *Achilles* of
1952, the great expanse of red subdues the ego and inspires a kind of tranquil awe. The non-painterliness of Newman's technique, however, prevents the spectator from indulging himself in sensation. By its dryness and banality, it draws attention away from the experience towards the idea.

Mark Rothko's soft, luminous palette is more sensuous than Newman's. Veils of thin pigment wash over the canvas and soak into it; warm colour lies over cool, cool over warm, dark over light, and light over dark. But sensuousness is not the same as hedonism. Rothko's colour fields have a contemplative intensity and invite a surrender of self. Among the ingredients of his art he listed: 'A clear preoccupation with death. All art deals with intimations of mortality.'

Born in Russia in 1903, Rothko emigrated wih his family to the United States at the age of ten, in 1913. Between 1921 and 1923 he studied at Yale University and attended Max Weber's drawing classes at the Art Students' League. In 1953 he was co-founder of the Ten, a group of Expressionistic artists who opposed the post-Cubist abstraction represented by American Abstract Artists. Before the war he painted human figures in deserted cityscapes.

In the early 1940s, like many of his contemporaries,
he experimented with automatism and Jungian bio-
morphism. He painted amalgams of human, plant,
animal and fish forms. His figures are arranged sche-
15 matically against soft light-filled grounds (*Entombment I*, 1946). They express, as Rothko said of an
early painting in this manner, 'a pantheism in which
man, bird, beast and tree – the known as well as the
unknowable – merge into a single tragic idea'.

Around 1947, that *annus mirabilis* of the New York School, Rothko exchanged his linear emblems for soft-focus blurs of colour, eventually reducing them to two or three roughly rectangular shapes stacked one on top of the other. At the same time he increased the size of his canvases and started to work on a monumental scale.

Although Rothko's compositions can be broken down into separate components, he found ways of preserving the integrity of the 'field'. There is no central point of attention. His rectangles fill the picture, the shape of which they repeat and confirm. Because of his use of wash the unifying texture of the canvas shows through. With a touch of irony, he encourages a contradiction between the illusion of a cloudy depth and the hard, visible fact of a surface.

17 The atmosphere of mature works such as *Red, White and Brown* of 1957 is passive and meditative. Opaque mists of disembodied colour invite the spectator into a quiet space, metaphorically equivalent to reverie. They express a not displeasing melancholy, close in feeling to Vergil's *sunt lacrimae rerum et mentem mortalia tangunt*: 'There are tears in the nature of things, and hearts are touched by transience.'

Rothko did not change this stylistic formula, but
his colours gradually darkened. Late canvases such
16 as *Black on Grey* are bleakly pessimistic. His life
ended in suicide in 1970.

Adolph Gottlieb's development followed the same pattern as Rothko's: mythic figuration yielded to abstract emblems on a blank ground. However, he did not go so fast or so far. Born in 1903 in New York, he trained at the Art Students' League, travelled through Europe and spent some time in Paris. During the 1930s he painted realistic views of the American scene. Under the impact of Surrealism and Freudian psychology, as well as Klee and Mondrian, Gottlieb devised a personal manner based on an irregular grid, containing images drawn from primitive art and parts of the human anatomy, for paintings which he called *Pictographs*. He adopted this name because 'it was necessary for me to utterly repudiate so-called "good painting" in order to express what was visually true for me'. Curiously, as his career progressed, he appears to have become increasingly concerned with technique. His pictures are tidy and personable and present themselves to their best advantage.

In the early 1950s, after a decade of *Pictographs*, Gottlieb rationalized his principles of composition:

18 as in *Frozen Sounds No. 1*, an earth-like band stretches across the lower part of the canvas, and in a pale 'sky' above hangs a row of ovoid or rectangular discs. Further reduction followed in 1957 with his *Burst* series. A single 'sun' now dominates the top half of the picture: it has a passivity which is in sharp contrast to the active linearity of the interlaced bundle of brushstrokes below. Gottlieb's observations on Gorky some years previously are a good description of his own *Bursts*: 'What he felt, I suppose, was a sense of polarity, not of dichotomy: that opposites could exist simultaneously within a body, within a painting or within an entire art.'

19 In a picture like *Brink*, painted in 1959, Gottlieb has nearly arrived at a colour field position. But his discs and exploding patches remain anecdotal incidents; he was willing to generalize and abstract the 'pictograph' or sign, but he refused to banish it altogether, whether by elimination (Newman) or magnification (Rothko). Cautious and consistent, Gottlieb stayed within what he knew until his death in 1974.

Clyfford Still is an artist of a more uncompromising frame of mind. His attitude to the avant-garde was as dismissive as that of Pollock's teacher, Benton; and, having passed through Bauhaus, Dada, Surrealist and Cubist phases, Still then obdurately turned his back on contemporary art movements. 'That ultimate in irony – the Armory Show of 1913 – had dumped on us the combined and sterile conclusions of European decadence,' was his final conclusion. In its place he cultivated a pioneering individualism – an attitude which, in its way, is as American as apple-pie. Art was a way of life, a matter of conscience: 'Hell, it's not just about painting – any fool can put colour on canvas.'

Still, born in North Dakota in 1904, studied at Spokane and Washington State universities, obtaining a master's degree in 1935, and spent six years as a teacher. The representational work he did during these years anticipates his later abstractions: a vertical figure stands in an open landscape, and there is a moral duality symbolized in sun and earth, light and dark.

Still moved to an early 'myth-making' manner which resembled that of Rothko and Gottlieb, although arrived at independently. In 1941 his artistic production was curtailed by war work; after a one-man show in San Francisco in 1943 he resumed full-time painting, and during the next few years he abandoned figuration for good. He did so with a characteristic decisiveness, saying later: 'I have no brief for signs or symbols or literary allusions in painting. They are crutches for illustrators and politicians desperate for an audience.'

Still devised a distinctive format to which he has
27,28 since kept. *Painting 1948-D, 1951 Yellow,* and
30 *Painting 1951* show a colour field corroded by torn
flame-like verticals. Still's designs are rationally organized and are, as Lawrence Alloway has observed, 'like the colour code of a map . . . that is turning back into a substantial reality; not a key to somewhere else, but itself a land'.

Although this is a useful metaphor, the reference to landscape should not be taken too literally. 'The fact that I grew up on the prairies has nothing to do with my paintings, with what people think they find in them,' Still said in an interview. 'I paint only myself, not nature.'

During the 1940s he reduced his originally brilliant chromaticism: his fields became black or opaque purple. Forms or pictorial disturbances which had occurred in the centre of the picture are pushed to the sides. Then, in the 1950s, an unexpected lyricism
29 makes an appearance, and in works like *Painting 1958*
colours seem more content to please than previously.

Still, like Newman, has an exalted notion of art. His aim is to purify the act of painting so that it can transcend itself and become a self-sufficient assertion of the sublime. He once compared the artist to a man who journeys through a wasted terrain and reaches a high plateau: 'Imagination, no longer fettered by the laws of fear, became as one with Vision. And the Act, intrinsic and absolute, was its meaning, and the bearer of its passion.'

Allies and Successors

Ad Reinhardt qualifies for no more than temporary membership of the New York School. He was at heart opposed to Abstract Expressionism; immediacy and indeterminacy were equally alien to him. The hieratic clarity of Eastern forms of expression was more to his way of thinking, and he sought the 'ultimate' painting that would be, like the Buddha image, 'breathless, timeless, styleless, lifeless, deathless, endless'. He admired Mondrian, rejected Surrealism, and ignored calligraphy: 'Nowhere in the world has it been clearer than in Asia that anything irrational, momentary, spontaneous, unconscious, primitive, expressionistic, accidental or informal cannot be called serious art.'

For most of his life Reinhardt adhered to a geometric form of abstraction, but in the 1940s he struck up friendships with Newman, Rothko and Still, and started to paint all-over canvases. These were composed at first of blurs and lines, then of small brushed
35 rectangles (*Painting*, 1950), and then of overlapping
36 horizontal rectangles with hard edges (*Red Painting*,
1952). By 1951 he was well on his way to the all-black *Ultimate Paintings* of his final minimal style, which, with their close values and barely discernible rectilinear divisions, are deliberately made almost impossible to reproduce.

Despite, or perhaps because of, their ambition to extend the frontiers of art and to carve a territory that would be all their own, the Abstract Expressionists wanted to know what it was that they were leaving. They listened eagerly to teachers and critics who could tell them of developments in Europe and provide them with working formulas they could apply to their own activities. Hans Hofmann took a lifelong interest in art education, and was also a distinguished painter, who ranks high in the second rank of the New York School. Born in Germany in 1880, he started out as a scientist (inventing a magnetic comptometer), also studied art, and settled in Paris between 1904 and 1914, meeting Matisse, Picasso and Braque, together with Delaunay, who taught him his colour theory. Hofmann founded his own art school in Munich in 1915. He emigrated to the United States in 1932, and soon opened another school in New York.

Hofmann's finest paintings summarize the conflicting achievements of early twentieth-century art within the context of an individual manner. He taught that 'creative expression is . . . the spiritual translation of inner concepts into form, resulting from the fusion of these intuitions with artistic means of expression in a unity of spirit and form'. Painting was 'forming with colour', and his interest, both pedagogic and creative, lay in finding a synthesis of Cubist structure and a Fauvist palette. (Clement Greenberg claimed that 'you could learn more about Matisse's colour [from Hofmann] than from Matisse himself'.)

Hofmann painted in a semi-abstract manner between 1936 and 1941; his subjects were always identifiable and were organized in brightly coloured, structured areas. From 1942 he swam with the tide, practising automatism and devising a biomorphic vocabulary of forms. He also invented an original drip and splash technique (anticipating Pollock).

In 1946 Hofmann began the series of abstractions
20 for which he is best remembered. *Transfiguration*, of
1947, for instance, consists of energetically painted

areas with some linear elements. Traces of Cubist organization remain, but the design is held in balance by the 'push and pull' interaction between three-dimensional depth and two-dimensional surface. 'Every movement releases a counter-movement,' he wrote. 'A represented form that does not owe its existence to a perception of movement is not a form.' In the 1950s Hofmann experimented with many different modes of expression. In some canvases, such
22 as *Fantasia in Blue*, rectangles overloaded with richly coloured pigment are placed among free gestural areas, and in others, towards 1960 and after, such as
21 *Rising Moon*, broad semi-transparent washes glow from a white ground.

Robert Motherwell is another New York artist with a distinctively European bent. Born in 1915, he entered Stanford University and later Harvard, where he studied art history. He took a somewhat dilettante view of culture and the good life, and lamented the disappearance of 'the wonderful things of the past – the late afternoon encounters, the leisurely repasts, the discriminations of taste, the graces of manners, and the gratuitous cultivation of minds'.

In 1940 he met the Surrealists-in-exile, and, as well as introducing him to automatism and Freudian psychology, they confirmed his instinct for nineteenth-century French aesthetics. Leaning on Baudelaire's theory of correspondences, according to which 'scents, colours and sounds respond to one another', Motherwell held that complete abstraction was impossible: 'The "pure" red of which certain abstractionists speak does not exist. Any red is rooted in blood, glass, wine, hunter's caps and a thousand other concrete phenomena.'

Motherwell experimented with collage, and his early works are influenced by Picasso, Matisse and Schwitters; but his first major paintings, the series
26 entitled *Elegies to the Spanish Republic*, were begun in 1949 (by 1965, he had finished more than a hun-

dred). Vertical rectangles and ovals spread across these long frieze-like canvases. The colouring is usually black on white. According to Motherwell, 'the pictures are . . . general metaphors for life and death, and their interrelation'. This Freudian conjunction of Eros and Thanatos is one of his characteristic themes, and is here indicated by the phallic configuration of his forms.

There are other oppositions in Motherwell's work: figure and ground edges overlap so that both are grafted into a unified surface, and gesture and field (flat planes and a simple monumentality, recalling colour field abstraction), are handled in painterly fashion with random drips and splashes.

Motherwell often paints on an intimate scale, as in
25 his *Je t'aime* series during the mid-1950s; but his unique contribution lies in the intimacy and personal feeling with which he can fill a monumental canvas.

Around 1950, emboldened by the success of Pollock and his fellow-pioneers, four painters abandoned figuration for Abstract Expressionism. They were none of them young men, and they had spent their careers working in traditional styles.

Franz Kline, born in 1910, trained in painting at Boston University and spent a few years in England. Until the late 1940s he produced studies of city scenes. Then, quite suddenly, he switched to gestural black-and-white canvases, which look as if they are gigantic enlargements of ideograms. In fact, the resemblance to Oriental calligraphy is misleading: 'people sometimes think I take a white canvas and paint a black sign on it, but this is not true. I paint the white as well as the black, and the white is just as important.'

Kline's compositions are abstract, but they reflect the patterns of urban landscape: 'If someone says, "That looks like a bridge," it doesn't bother me really. A lot of them do. . . . I think that if you use long lines, they become – what could they be? The

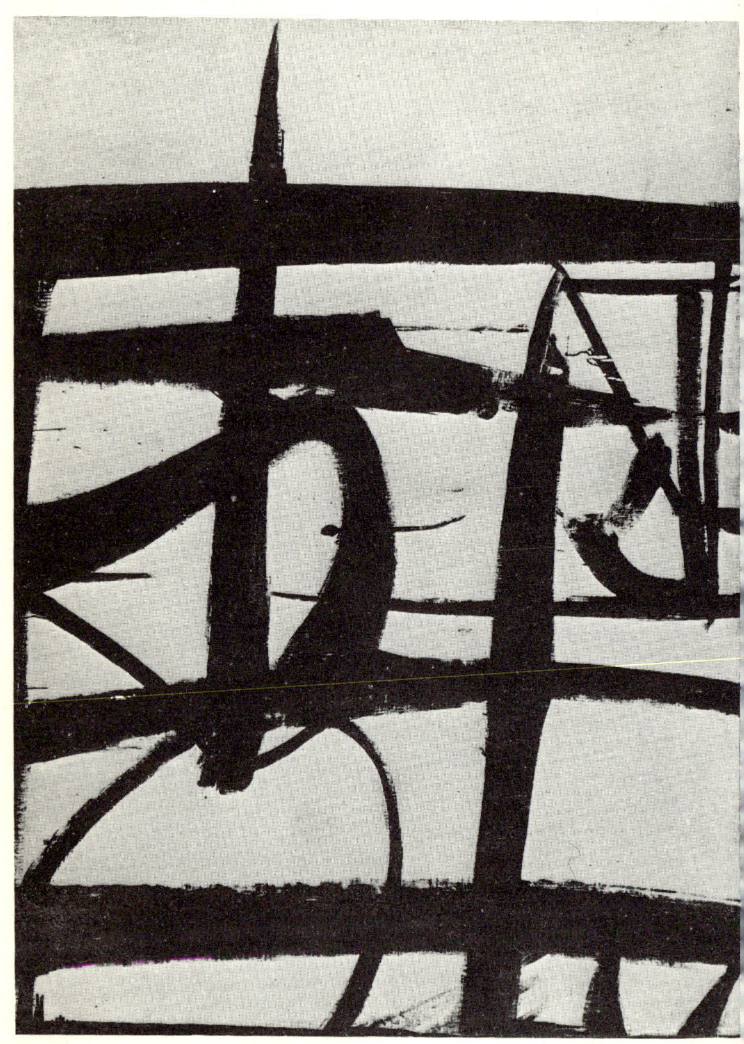

Franz Kline. *Cardinal,* 1950. Oil on canvas, $77\frac{5}{8} \times 56\frac{3}{4}$ (197.8 × 144.2). Collection George and Elinor Poindexter, New York.

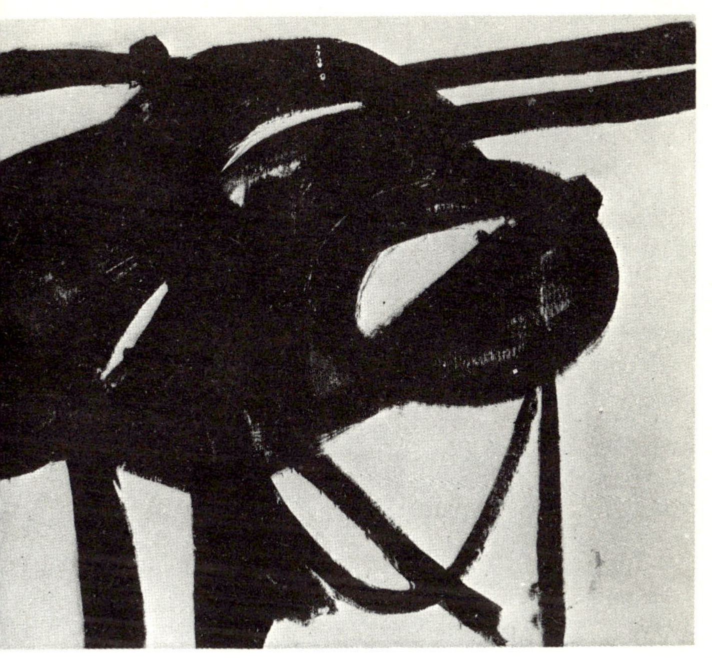

Franz Kline. *Chief*, 1950. Oil on canvas, $58\frac{3}{8} \times 73\frac{1}{2}$ (148.3 × 186.7). The Museum of Modern Art, New York. Gift of Mr and Mrs David M. Solinger.

only thing they could be is either highways or bridges.'

Kline's work at its best conveys a sense of barely controlled excitement with the act of painting. As he puts it, 'Paint never seems to behave the same. Even the same paint doesn't, you know. It doesn't dry the same. It doesn't stay and look at you the same way.' Corrections, erasures and overpainting give the spectator the impression that he is himself taking part in the creative process: Kline seems to be, as he said of Bonnard, 'organizing in front of you'.

In the last years of his life, his pictures became blacker and more atmospheric. Kline also began to

24 experiment with colour: but *King Oliver*, for instance, fine as it is, is only the old monochrome Kline translated, and he did not find his way to an authentic chromaticism before his comparatively early death in 1962.

Philip Guston was born in Canada in 1913 and studied at the Otis Art Institute in Los Angeles. He visited Mexico to see the murals of Rivera and his colleagues, and evolved a figurative style in which memory played an essential part: painting was 'a tug-of-war between what you know and what you don't know'.

In 1951 he embraced abstraction, but never supposed that this meant the complete abolition of subject matter: 'There is something ridiculous and miserly in the myth we inherit from abstract art: that painting is autonomous, pure and for itself, and therefore we habitually analyze its ingredients and define its limits. But painting is "impure". We are image-makers and image-ridden.'

For a while Guston deployed hatched brushstrokes vertically and horizontally on the canvas (a recollection of Mondrian); his colours were hesitant, pastel and luminous, and he was nicknamed an Abstract Impressionist on account of their atmospheric lyricism. From 1954, however, he painted in larger but less geometric areas, using a sombre palette and bolder brushwork. Later still, there is a partial return
41 to representation: half-identifiable objects emerge from the paint surface – traces of old forgotten things which the mind cannot quite recall.

For James Brooks, Pollock was as gigantic a figure as Picasso or Matisse. The great drip paintings had the same liberating effect on Brooks in his middle age that Cubism had had on him as a young man. Born in St Louis, Mo., in 1906, he studied at the Southern Methodist University and the Dallas Art Institute. In the 1930s he was associated with the Regionalist movement (although he did not repudiate European modernism), and the area where he grew up provided him with his main source of inspiration. From Picasso he learnt how to abstract from nature while preserving a recognizable image. He became well known as a muralist.

After discharge from military service in 1945, Brooks explored Cubism and then started looking for ways to loosen the closed structure of his compositions; Pollock's automatism gave him the cue he needed. He painted the backs of his canvases, and cautiously worked and re-worked the chance patterns that had soaked through into subtle, integrated
40 rhythms. The end-product, as in the *No. 36* of 1950, is a shifting flux of transparent zones threaded with thin lines. In 1953 his pigmentation increased in density, and large gestural forms jostled for attention, gently pulling and pushing against one another.

Bradley Walker Tomlin was born in 1899, brought up in New York, and educated at the College of Fine Arts of Syracuse University. He earned a living as an illustrator and also painted murals. Little of his early work survives. From about 1939 he adopted a decorative Cubism into which straightforwardly representational elements are incorporated. A dreamy symbolism takes first place over design. After 1945 he became friendly with Gottlieb, whose example persuaded him to introduce more spontaneity into his pictures. He painted white calligraphic signs on a black ground, but feeling uncomfortable without a linear structure went on to transform them into curved
39 bands fitted together in a loose grid. In *No. 20* (1949), during his final period, these bands were reduced to small rectangular dabs. Tomlin's gentle, melancholy canvases are evidence that gesture painting was able to accommodate passivity and elegance.

During the 1950s critics, collectors, museums, and the public at large realized that they now had to reckon with an American art of world stature. Artists became rich and famous, and painting was no longer a career for congenital 'loft rats'. In a sense this made life difficult for new arrivals on the scene. The major discoveries had all been made, and the desperate pressures against which the Abstract Expressionists had so heroically and successfully reacted no longer existed. Reforming zeal was, therefore, out of place, and young artists adopted a cool, uncommitted stance. Rather than Pollock or De Kooning, they took the colour field painters, Newman and Still, as their point of departure. However, they were more interested in the minimality of colour field art than in its pursuit of the sublime; and they agreed with Reinhardt's insistence on anonymity and the absence of emotion.

Nevertheless, a few continued to offer gestural abstraction, usually in terms of colour. Helen Frankenthaler (born 1928), who married Robert Motherwell, developed a staining technique that derived from Pollock's drip paintings and from Rothko's dyed washes. The autographic brushstroke
42 disappears, and pictures such as *Blue Territory* express an impersonal delight in pure colour, light-filled and arranged in free, accidental patterns. In 1952 Morris Louis (1912–62) came across Pollock's work and met Helen Frankenthaler, who introduced
37 him to staining. In his series known as *Veils*, diaphanous colour curtains flow over one another: later, in the *Unfurled* series, diagonal rivulets of brilliant colour pour down the lower corners of otherwise untouched canvases. This was followed by the *Stripe*
38 or *Pillar* paintings which codify colour into striped fasces or bundles. Louis metamorphosed his Abstract Expressionist inheritance: pigment has become optical and insubstantial, and the wandering edges of his forms are determined only by the drying process. Colour speaks for itself released from the artist's intentions.

The painting of Louis and Frankenthaler is a far cry from the frontiersman hacking his way into new territories and surveying the canvas as if it were an empty land on which to impose his will. Only a few years after their triumphs, the Abstract Expressionists appeared as remote as the Founding Fathers of the Republic. Their successors paid them due respect and admiration, but the adventure was over. Consolidation does not require the same skills as conquest.

Europe

The independent growth of gestural abstraction on both sides of the Atlantic is not as remarkable a phenomenon as it seems at first sight. Simultaneity of invention is common in the sciences; when conditions are broadly the same in different parts of the wood, there is nothing surprising in a coincidence of brush fires.

Immediately after the Second World War, Europe and America shared the inheritance of Cubism and Surrealism, the post-war malaise, and the crisis of subject matter. Accordingly, the principles of the new European Abstract art, variously known as Informal Art (or *art informel*), Lyrical Abstraction and Tachism, had a good deal in common with those of the New York School: there was plenty of talk about spontaneity of technique, liberation from the old formal conventions, cultivation of the unconscious, and the rejection of illusionistic space.

Nevertheless, the resemblances conceal varying objectives. Europe – its artistic life still centred on Paris – was less radical than America. Thus, Pollock
45 and his European contemporary Jean Dubuffet were both excited by the potential of unfamiliar materials and techniques. Just as the one poured fluid paint on the canvas, mixing it with 'sand, broken glass and other foreign matter', the other built up his impasto with plaster, glue, putty and asphalt. However, Dubuffet's attention was fixed on the materials them-

selves ('I do my best to rehabilitate objects regarded as unpleasing'); Pollock, on the other hand, was only concerned with facilitating the creative act. Again, we do not find in Europe the repudiation of easel painting by enlargement of scale: there is no all-over colour field.

This said, the triumph of the United States has led to an under-valuation of the post-war School of Paris, or at least of its leading figures. Clement Greenberg summed up the New York orthodoxy in 1953: 'For all the adventurousness of their "images", the latest generation in Paris still go in for "paint quality" in the accepted sense. They "enrich" the surface with films of oil or varnish, or with buttery paint. Also, they tend to tailor the design so that it hits the eye with a certain patness: or else the unity of the picture is made to depend on a semblance of the old kind of illusion of depth obtained through glazing or tempered colour.'

This critique, acute as it is, does not do justice to the major talents. Georges Mathieu, painter and leading publicist of Lyrical Abstraction, protested at the animosity of the Abstract Expressionists in America: 'I have been surprised that in New York you had not immediately recognized Wols as the Rimbaud of painting. I do not want to believe that a narrow-minded nationalism has had anything to do with the reserves you showed at the time of his exhibit.'

Wols was the *nom de guerre* of Wolfgang Schulze. Born in Berlin in 1913, he was a skilled violinist and photographer as well as a student of zoology, geology, botany and ethnology. He never saw painting as a profession, and as far as possible avoided the world of dealers and exhibitions. In his youth he came into contact with Paul Klee, Otto Dix and George Grosz, all of whom, especially Klee, influenced his work. Disgusted by the Nazis, he left Germany in 1932 and settled in Spain until he was deported to

France in 1936. His early watercolours and drawings are elaborate automatist doodles. However, Wols's playfully horrific grotesques are marked by an Expressionistic and German anguish as well as a Surrealistic spontaneity and wit.

The Second World War and the German occupation confirmed him in his pessimistic view of life. He drew some comfort from observing the forms of nature ('the stones, the fish/The rocks seen through a glass/The sea-salt and the sky/Have made me forget the importance of man'). In his drawings organic shapes merge with imaginary biomorphs suggested by the half-awake mind (he used to close his eyes and let involuntary hypnogogic images form on his lids). They convey a queasy, perturbing eroticism.

Wols worked on a small scale: 'the movements of the hand and fingers suffice to express everything. The arm movements necessary in painting a canvas involve too much ambitious purpose and gymnastics.' Nevertheless, by the mid-1940s he was ready for a change. At the suggestion of a gallery owner he launched, almost against his will, on a sequence of paintings, executed rapidly and in something approaching a hypnotic state over a period of a few
44 months. In *Composition V*, painted in 1946, Wols has achieved his mature style. His brushwork is free, gestural and unplanned, and his use of colour creates a vague, uncertain space, an arena in which he can trace his familiar threaded squiggles. Although the imagery is abstract and intuitive, there are intimations of a microscopic molecular universe.

Like Pollock, Wols was an adventurer who used his art as a vehicle for self-revelation. His eccentric, Bohemian life-style was itself a creative achievement, in (as Mathieu suggests) the Rimbaudian vein. Alcoholism led to an early death in 1951; but his bleak career was felt to be a success in the Existentialist sense of the assertion of existence through action, and was extremely influential during the 1950s.

Jean Dubuffet was the second major figure to emerge in post-war France. Fascinated by the painting of children, psychotics and amateurs, he coined the term *art brut* (i.e. raw, untreated or crude art) to define its rough-and-ready anti-art quality: 'I hold to be useless those types of acquired skill and those gifts (such as we are used to finding in the works of professional painters) whose sole effect seems to me to be that of extinguishing all spontaneity, switching off and condemning the work to inefficacy.'

Born in 1901 in Le Havre, Dubuffet moved in his teens to Paris where he studied art for a time and also occupied himself with literature, music, philosophy and languages. In 1924 he gave up painting, and apart from a brief interlude in Buenos Aires as an industrial designer spent most of the next two decades in the wine business. He did not paint full-time again until 1942. Two years later he held an exhibition in Paris in which he showed Klee-like images of houses, still-lifes and other representational scenes, all as if drawn by a child. They embody a certain messiness, a *maladresse anti-plastique*; the term implies a *rejection* of the concern with 'paint quality' of which Greenberg accuses the School of Paris.

Dubuffet held another exhibition in 1946, 'Mirobolus, Macadam & Cie., Hautes Pâtes', a title intended to evoke the magical 'naïveté of the street conjuror'. It was now that he began experimenting with new materials, making a paste he could play with like a child with plasticine. He was moved by the unnoticed poetry of everyday objects, especially those without formal properties, such as dust or walls. In the early 1950s Dubuffet launched three new series, the *Ladies' Bodies*, large female figures with primitive fertility associations, and *Soil and Ground* and *Radiant Land* in which 'friendly animals and nice little men' are set against backgrounds suggesting geological structures and fossils.

45 In *Table, Constant Companion*, painted in 1953, a flat frontal image is richly textured. If the figure is a table, it also has animal associations, looking rather like a headless and tailless elephant. However, Dubuffet's delight in materials and his whimsical simplicity of form indicate that he is not primarily concerned with representation. He occupies a position somewhere between figuration and abstraction, where the 'thisness' or physical presence of his canvases is as significant as the child-like bestiary with which he peoples them. In 1956, Dubuffet evolved a new technique based on collage: he cut small pieces from painted fabric – stars, discs and lozenges – and stuck them on to the canvas in a mosaic, sometimes adding bits of tinfoil, dried flowers or leaves.

New approaches to the physical 'matter' (or *matière*) of painting are found in the work of many Europeans who wished, like Dubuffet, not only to widen their expressive scope but also to attack the conventions of 'fine art'. Antoni Tàpies, born in Barcelona in 1923, adopted a matter-based style in 1953, using a mixture of glue, plaster of Paris and sand. His motives included a despair with the industrial present and a yearning for the 'natural'. Tàpies, who insists that art must have a 'moral substratum', aims to remind man of his real nature not by large statements but gentle specific reminders. His admiring comment on Anton Chekhov sums up his own intentions: 'It's extraordinary, he tells you almost nothing. He is almost absent. He gives you bits of reality in its raw state, which cross his mind.'

50 In *White and Orange*, painted in 1967, Tàpies, like Dubuffet, gives the painting the substantiality of a wall (his name, by a coincidence which pleases him, means 'walls' in Catalan), and a symmetrical design has been scored and gouged into the thick plastered surface. In other works, by dialectical contrast, formal balance is either eliminated or submerged in spontaneous gestural techniques, including a manner of

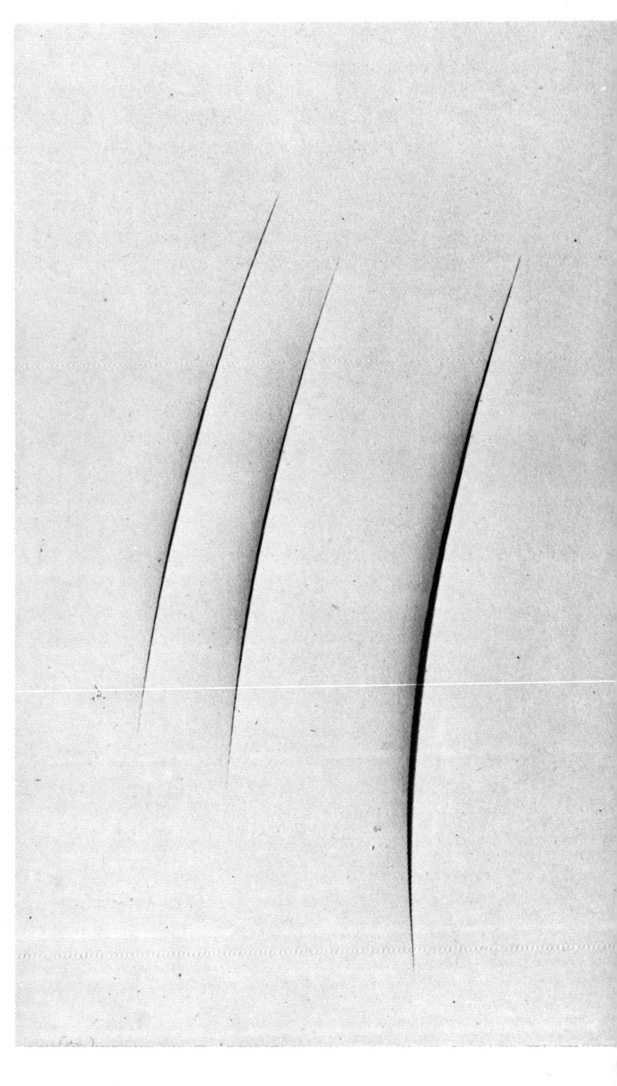

Lucio Fontana. *Spatial Concept,* 1960. Canvas, $38\frac{1}{4} \times 23\frac{1}{2}$ (96.6×59.7). McRoberts & Tunnard Ltd, London.

painting – and overpainting – that shows an awareness of the New York School. Tàpies' attempt to make the canvas a concrete object is weakened by an underlying illusionism (*White and Orange* sets out to look like a wall, but isn't), and he has gone some way to solve this problem in recent years by incorporating real objects in his work, such as baskets, furniture and pieces of wood, and transforming them into whimsical, quietly Surrealistic assemblages.

The Italian artist Antonio Burri, born in 1915, handles – or, to be precise, damages – ready-made materials. He is best known for his *Sacks*, in which he creates a design from pieces of sacking and cloth; he has also produced collages from metal, wood and
49 packaging. In *Sack No. 5*, painted in 1953, the holes in the sacking and the dark ground recall bandaged wounds and derive from what he saw as a medical officer during the Second World War. Burri's pictures are a melancholy, partly autobiographical critique of the age; unfortunately, they manage to be neat and pretty – too much so to convey a powerful emotional charge.

Another Italian, Lucio Fontana (born in Argentina in 1899; he died in Italy in 1969), has been grouped with the matter painters. His matter was the canvas itself, often monochrome, which he slashed or gouged. In these literal ways he opened up the picture plane: the spectator can see through it to three-dimensional space beyond, which itself becomes an element of the composition. Fontana's destructive methods may also be taken as an ironic dismissal of easel painting; and they record with some precision a gesture – namely, cutting with a knife. However, in 1946 he issued his *White Manifesto*, in which he makes it clear that perception and the sensation of perception are his primary concerns: 'We need an art which draws its value from itself, and not from any ideas we might have about it. Colour and sound are found in nature, and linked with matter. Matter, colour and sound – these are the phenomena whose simultaneous evolution forms an integral part of the new art.'

Elsewhere in the document Fontana observes that 'sensation' was everything in primitive art: 'it is our intention to develop this original condition of man'. From the mid-1940s Fontana's work became increasingly sculptural, and he experimented with relatively unorthodox media – such as electric light – in his pursuit of a total 'synthesis' of colour, sound, movement, time and space.

In France, a number of artists confirmed the matter painting of Dubuffet and the Informalism of Wols more directly. Jean Fautrier, born in 1897,
43 attracted attention with his series of *Hostages*. He used a gluey paste made from cement, plaster and paint which he applied with a palette knife. Vague human forms or faces, which are built up from layer after layer of whitish-coloured pigment, float against a blurred opalescent ground. These images refer to some executions Fautrier witnessed during the war. In his later work, though, the significance of his subject matter became more cryptic, and he widened it to include objects, nudes and landscapes – semi-abstract and only just identifiable. He also produced completely abstract pictures. As a rule, his compositions are dominated by a flat central image.

Jean-Paul Riopelle is a Canadian painter and sculptor, born in Quebec in 1922. He was influenced by the Surrealists and met Wols and several like-minded French Informalists in 1945. His work has its roots in an affection for landscape; and by the end of the 1940s he had developed a 'non-figurative pantheism'. Technically, he became interested in texture and broke down his designs into small brightly coloured patches irradiated by thin lines of
46 force. This gives such works as *Painting* (1951–52) an all-over quality, although modified by atmospheric spatial effects and a palette that evokes the colours of

nature. A growing preoccupation with mass in space has led Riopelle in recent years to a series of sculptural experiments.

If matter is one dimension of the post-war School of Paris, gesture is another. The brushmark or the calligraphic sign – seen as a record of psychic activity – was a sufficient content. This entailed an emphasis on 'the act of painting'; but, in contrast with the United States, it was seldom whole-hearted. For Ecole de Paris painters it was a means of making new kinds of design which they could isolate and lovingly preserve, or exploit for decorative effect.

Hans Hartung was born in Leipzig in 1904, and it was not until 1935, after numerous vicissitudes, that he settled in Paris. During his formative years, he had been influenced by Kandinsky and Klee. Following active service in the war (he was wounded and lost a leg), he became a French citizen. His work is consistently marked by what Klee called 'psychic improvisation'. His mature style, from 1934 on, depends on a nervous, automatist manner and owes a good deal to Oriental art. Painting for him is a kind of abstract sign language in which human psychomotor energies are translated into concrete form. In 1947 he observed, using an interesting analogy (compare Tobey, p. 14), that 'Our contemporaries, or the generations to come, will learn to read, and one day this direct writing will be found more normal than figurative painting, just as we find our alphabet – abstract and unlimited in its possibilities – more rational than the figurative writing of the Chinese.'

After 1954 his paintings became increasingly Informal: they record without embarrassment the artist's second thoughts. Hartung treats a smooth blank ground as a field for the expression of energy. Spiralling networks and meshes of coloured line create a variable rhythmic depth. In time Hartung's self-confidence grew, and his later canvases are distinguished by a controlled technical virtuosity.

His designs look more and more like practised ideo-
47 grams. There is little indecision in *T1958–4*: instead,
routine vitality framed within a tidy, contained
image. For all their energy, Hartung's brushmarks
seem neutralized, like flies in amber.

Hartung has frequently been compared with Pierre
Soulages, whose compositions are made up from a
lattice of broad black bands, like the enlarged strokes
of a housepainter's brush. Born in 1919 in France, his
early interests were in prehistoric and Romanesque
art. He was impressed by exhibitions of Cézanne and
Picasso which he saw in 1938–39. After 1946 he
began to exhibit in Paris. Although, like many of his
contemporaries, Soulages was attracted to gesture, to
the wide sweep of the arm across the canvas, this was
more for the architectonic possibilities which it
offered than for the excitement of movement. His
48 pictures, of which *Painting* (1959) is a characteristic
example, follow a rational programme: a framework
of black bands is painted on a more or less plain,
brightly coloured ground, and this, in turn, is over-
laid with folding vertical or diagonal bands. The
result is a gravely monumental structure: the upper
levels set up dynamic formal and spatial rhythms, but
these are firmly contained within the lower ones.
Such formality contrasts with the more spontaneous
24 gestures of, say, Kline's *King Oliver* (1958). Soulages
was firm in his commitment to abstraction itself: 'I
do not start from an object or from a landscape with
a view to distorting them, nor, conversely, do I seek,
as I paint, to provoke their appearance.' (Compare,
again, Kline's easy-going attitude, p. 35–37).

Georges Mathieu, born in 1921, was one of the earliest Frenchmen to appreciate the significance of the New York School, and has been a tireless propagandist for what he refers to as Lyrical Abstraction. He admires the art of the age of Louis XIV, and seems to have seen his role as that of an arbiter of taste, a contemporary Le Brun. A great organizer of exhibitions and publisher of manifestos, usually formulated in high rhetorical terms, he began to paint in 1942, under the Surrealist influence of Matta and Masson. Deeply moved by paintings of Wols which he saw in 1947, he soon developed his own personal style. Both in principle and in practice he was close to the Abstract Expressionists. He talked of 'the intrinsic autonomy of the work of art', and of the 'phenomenology of the "very act of painting"'.

Mathieu believes that conscious intention is best expelled from painting by an extreme rapidity of execution. He has painted in public on a number of occasions, and in Tokyo he once completed a canvas over twelve metres long in less than twenty minutes. However, except for some early works, his pictures
60 are more decorative than aggressive: as in *Mathieu from Alsace . . .*, lacerics of bright pigment (red, white, black and blue are his favourite colours) stretch horizontally across the middle of the pictures or spread out from a central coagulation of pigment like overpainted Chinese characters. Because they keep a good distance from the edges of the canvas, they do not function as an all-over field. Mathieu's work has an appealing *joie de vivre*, although his real achievement lies in the field of publicity.

Henri Michaux, born in Belgium in 1899, has moved freely throughout his life between literature and visual art. His preferred medium is ink on paper, and painting is for him a non-verbal extension of writing – a carrying on of poetry by other means. Like Hartung and Mathieu, he was influenced by Oriental calligraphy; and he speaks of being 'possessed by movements, completely tensed by these forms which came at me full speed, in rhythmic succession'. This is a good summary of his drawing technique; blots (*taches*) pour on to the paper in quick succession, under the pressure of emotion and, on occasion, mescalin. As in *Painting in India Ink*, of 1966, these blots come together into a field of energy, which the eye can read, passing from one small expressive sign to another.

A host of subsidiary figures complicate the post-
war Parisian art scene. Many had been working in
figurative styles in the 1930s, and their early concerns
informed their later manners. Jean Bazaine, born in
1904, moved in his forties from a representational
post-Cubist position towards a free abstraction in-
51 spired by nature, as in *Child and the Night* (1949). An
original feature of his work is that his compositions
seem to pour over the edge of the canvas and so
subvert its arbitrary rectangularity. Alfred Manessier,
born in 1911, has followed much the same course as
Bazaine, ending up with a symbolic, landscape-based
abstraction which expresses a mystical Christian
52 viewpoint; a typical title is *Night in Gethsemane*. His
finest work is in stained glass. Maurice Estève, born
in 1904, passed through most phases of modern art
before devising his own variant of free abstraction,
in which painterly but static compositions are
assembled and unified by a rich palette. Although he
56 has been defined as a colourist, a work like *Friselune*
(1958) also has a constructed planar quality deriving
from Cézanne.

Nicolas de Staël was born in St Petersburg in 1914
and lived mostly in Belgium and France until his
suicide in 1950. By his economical illusionism and his
decorative palette, De Staël achieved considerable
popularity. But he was never a painter's painter, and
made comparatively little impression on his contemporaries or successors. His career is of interest because
it reflects an unwillingness to make a complete commitment either to abstraction or to figuration. Not
unlike the *Nocturnes* of Whistler, his vividly coloured
designs read equally well as harmonious arrange-
ments of pure form or as stylized but atmospheric
evocations of landscape. In one respect the tables are
turned: his titles, unlike Whistler's, suggest repre-
57 sentation (*Figure by the Sea*, 1952). Ambivalence

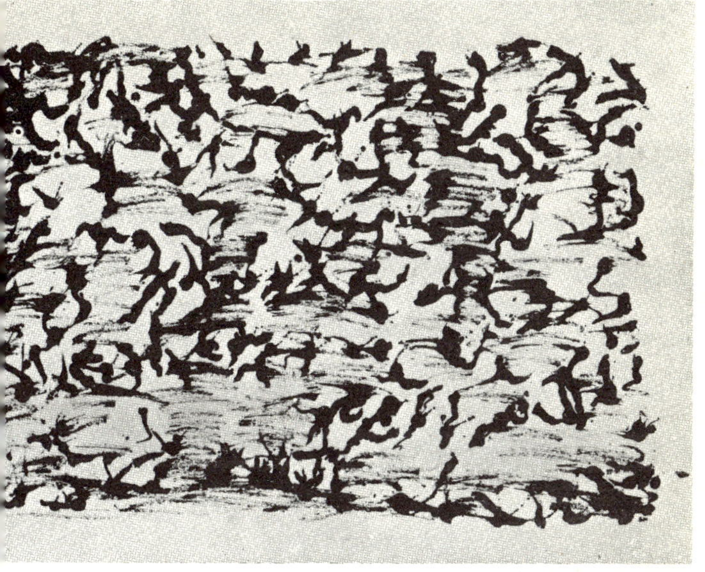

Henri Michaux. *Painting in India Ink,* 1966. Ink on paper, $29\frac{1}{2} \times 42\frac{1}{8}$ (75 × 107). Galerie Le Point Cardinal, Paris.

permeated De Staël's whole aesthetic approach: 'For myself, in order to develop, I need always to function differently, from one thing to another, without an *a priori* aesthetic. I lose contact with the canvas every moment and find it again and lose it. This is absolutely necessary, because I believe in accident – as soon as I feel too logical, this upsets me and I turn naturally to illogicality.'

The Surrealists and German Expressionists attracted a following in the smaller countries of Northern Europe. In the late 1930s some Danes harnessed automatism and a painterly manner to their national folklore, filling their canvases with the trolls, gods and dragons of Nordic mythology. This runic Expressionism was offered as a corrective to 'sterile abstraction'. It drew some support from painters in

Belgium and Holland. The movement was institutionalized when in 1948 a group of Danish, Belgian and Dutch artists in Paris formed 'Cobra' (named from the first letters of Copenhagen, Brussels and Amsterdam). They included Karel Appel, Constant, Corneille, Christian Dotremont, Asger Jorn and Philippe Noiret; they were joined later by Atlan, Pierre Alechinsky and the Germans Karl Otto Götz and Otto Piene.

A keynote of Cobra was a high-spirited violence both in terms of style and content. In the aftermath of war, its members saw themselves as resistance fighters for art. They delighted in expressive exaggeration: 'It is snowing colours,' said Dotremont. 'The colours are like a scream.'

The dominant figure was Asger Jorn, born in Jutland in 1911. With a background of automatist Surrealism, he saw the artist, in familiar terms, as a heroic individualist, and painting as an existential gesture: 'Art is the unique act of man or the unique in human actions.' Kandinsky, Mirò and Klee influenced his work; but Le Corbusier and Léger also impressed him by their rigorous simplifications. A linear technique slowly gave way to a savage painterliness, and at the height of his powers in the second half of the 1950s, Jorn applied pigment in broad
53 bands and blotches of luminous colour (*Unlimited*, 1959–60). He never altogether abandoned his obsession with myth, and the hallucinatory images of legend lurk within his disturbed, swirling compositions.

Corneille, born Cornelis van Beverloo in Belgium in 1922, studied drawing in Amsterdam. His inspiration is drawn from landscape, and his Informal Abstractionist paintings are tranquil and cheerful, especially in comparison with his excitable colleagues. His early work is indebted to Mirò and Picasso. He adopted a novel means of abstracting landscape, taking a bird's eye view and presenting a flat patchwork of warm colours rather like an aerial
54

59 photograph of fields. The *Play of Sun on Waves* of 1958 can be recognized as a gestural seascape. More recently he has lightened his palette and produces more fluid designs.

Karel Appel, born in Amsterdam in 1921, is intoxicated by the process of painting, which he regards as a 'tangible sensuous experience'. He has been nicknamed the 'wild beast of colour': not altogether an accidental echo of 'Fauve', for he takes a Matisse-like joy in brilliant primary colour. However, his immediate antecedents were Jorn and his own compatriot De Kooning. His technique, as in the fiery *Two*
55 *Heads in a Landscape* of 1958, is extremely vigorous: 'My paint tube is like a rocket which describes its own space.' His figures, especially his nudes, have a fetishistic quality which owes something to primitive art and recalls the spontaneity of children's painting.

British painters, having cultural associations both with the mainland of Europe and the United States, were in a particularly strong position during the transitional post-war period when the leadership of contemporary art was passing from Paris to New York. The St Ives Group came together in the early 1940s round two senior figures, the sculptress Barbara Hepworth and the painter Ben Nicholson, and included Terry Frost, Patrick Heron, Roger Hilton and Peter Lanyon. Although they worked in very different styles, they had in common an interest in abstracting landscape and visual impressions. They exchanged their French heritage for a tactful Abstract Expressionism. It is interesting to observe how William Scott, born in 1913 in Scotland, shifted his allegiance from Gauguin and Cézanne to Rothko and other members of the New York School, and after a visit to New York in 1953 began to open up his canvases into broad 'fields' occupied by flat, symbolic forms.

Patrick Heron, born in Leeds in 1920, was another who was encouraged by the reductive example of the

American painting. In his paintings, flat, undifferen-
58 tiated shapes hover against plain grounds (*Manganese
in Deep Violet*, January 1967); sharp contrasts of
brilliant colour, equalized in intensity, stimulate
optical figure/field reversals, and create a visually
ambiguous depth.

Alan Davie, another Scot, born in 1920, has always
stood apart from the mainstream of British art. For
one thing, he identifies himself more firmly than
most with the elevated European concept of the role
of the artist. His comment that 'the artist was the first
magician and the first spiritual leader, and indeed
today must take the role of arch-priest of the new
spiritualism', has a Rimbaudian ring. Davie's gestural
élan and his liberating sense of colour sets him beside
the Cobra group as well as reflecting his discovery of
Pollock. However, his main interest is in colour-space
relationships which are articulated in structural
54 terms, in a highly individual manner (*Heavenly
Bridge No. 3*, 1960). His solid international reputation
bears witness to the precision with which he exem-
plifies the preoccupations of his age.

In a statement of his artistic aims in 1960, Davie identified the general direction in which he and his contemporaries on both sides of the Atlantic were, in their various ways, moving: 'I paint because I have nothing, or I paint because I am full of paint ideas, or I paint because I want a purple picture on my wall, or I paint because after I last painted, something appeared miraculously out of it . . . something strange, and maybe something strange may happen again.'

Glossary

Abstract Expressionism is the term applied specifically to those American painters, discussed on pp. 11–39 of this book, who developed a style of painting based on the free, expressive use of colour and on an attempt at spontaneous depiction of the imagery of the unconscious; their later work combines this expressionism with abstraction (the absence of imagery) in works which present all-over configuration (or fields) on a scale which dwarfs the spectator. The marks on the canvas serve as records of the gesture, the 'act of painting'. The all-over field later took the form, in the work of such artists as Newman, of a colour field (see below). The relationship between European and American painting in this vein is discussed here on pp. 5–6, 41–42. See the definitions below. The varied terminology reflects differences of usage rather than distinctions of meaning.

Action Painting is an alternative term to describe abstract or semi-abstract paintings dominated by the traces of bold arm gestures; known in Europe as Gestural Abstraction.

Art Brut (raw or crude art) is Jean Dubuffet's expression for the spontaneous art of psychotics, children and those who scrawl on walls.

Art Informel (Informal Art) is a term used on the continent of Europe to denote an art based on 'psychic improvisation'; the implication is that what is produced is the trace of a gesture rather than a material shape.

Colour field: the large-scale all-over field of Abstract Expressionism when it appears, as it does in the work of Newman and Still, without gestural marks or all-over configuration.

Gestural abstraction is any abstract art based on the record of a 'gesture' made by the artist as he paints.

Lyrical Abstraction is the term most commonly used to denote the post-war painting in Europe which corresponds to Action Painting in the USA. It combines free handling of paint, the rejection of geometrical abstraction and an interest in simple images derived from the unconscious. Dubuffet, Fautrier, Mathieu and Wols were held to be its leading exponents.

Matière (Matter) painting is any form of gestural abstraction which appears to do violence in some way to the materials used by the artist (Fontana, Tàpies, Burri).

Tachism (from *tache,* 'blot' or 'stain') is a term which has been used, pejoratively, to describe the Fauves and the Impressionists. In the 1940s it came to be synonymous with Action Painting. It equates the painter's mark with the ritual act of painting, and has been applied both to Frenchmen such as Michaux and to Americans such as Pollock.

Chronology

1933 Washington: President Roosevelt's New Deal Administration founds the Public Works of Art Project which gives employment to American artists. New York: Hans Hofmann opens his school of art; Mark Rothko has his first one-man show.

1935 Washington: The Federal Arts Project extends the principles of the PWAP. New York: Adolph Gottlieb and Rothko help found The Ten, a group wishing to combine 'a social consciousness with an abstract, expressionistic heritage'.

1936 New York: Josef Albers founds American Abstract Artists. Paris: Wols arrives in France.

1940 Fall of France. Leading Surrealists and other artists emigrate to New York, including Breton, Dali, Ernst, Chagall, Léger, Lipchitz, Masson, Matta, Mondrian, Tanguy and Zadkine.

1941 New York: Gottlieb begins his *Pictograph* series.

1941–42 New York: Gottlieb, Motherwell, Pollock and Rothko experiment with automatism. This leads in the course of time to myth-based paintings.

1942 Paris: Dubuffet resumes full-time painting after an interval of many years. Fautrier paints his *Hostages* series. New York: De Kooning experiments with automatism.

1943 New York: Gorky achieves his mature style with the *Garden of Sochi* series. San Francisco: Clyfford Still resumes painting after an interval caused by the war and has his first one-man show.

1944 New York: Baziotes shows at the Art of This Century Gallery; Hofmann innovates a 'drip' technique of painting. Paris: Dubuffet has his first exhibition.

1946 New York: Hofmann begins his 'push and pull' abstractions. Paris: Hartung takes French citizenship.

1947 New York: Pollock begins his 'drip' paintings. De Kooning paints his black and white abstractions in commercial paints. Still exhibits his first colour-field abstractions. Baziotes, Motherwell, Barnett Newman and Rothko are among the founders of The Subjects of the Artist, which led to the later Club meetings of the Abstract Expressionists. About this time, Rothko adopts his mature style, in which soft rectangles hover in space. Paris: Georges Mathieu stages *L'Imaginaire*, an exhibition of Lyrical Abstraction.

1948 New York: Gorky kills himself. Newman enters his colour-field manner. Paris: the Cobra Group is formed.

1949 New York: Motherwell begins his *Elegies to the Spanish Republic* (by 1955 he has completed more than a hundred). The Club is founded and becomes a focal point for Abstract Expressionist meetings and discussions.

1950 USA: About this time, Franz Kline, James Brooks, Philip Guston and Bradley Walker Tomlin abandon figuration for an Abstract Expressionist manner. Paris: Pollock has his first European one-man show.

1951 New York: De Kooning begins his *Women* series. Frankenthaler is introduced to Pollock's work.

1952 USA: Gottlieb abandons his *Pictographs* for the *Imaginary Landscapes*. Morris Louis sees Pollock's 'drip' paintings and learns about staining from Frankenthaler.

1953 New York: Pollock abandons his drip technique. Spain: Antoni Tàpies begins his *matière* paintings.

1955 New York: De Kooning returns to abstraction.

1956 USA: Pollock dies in a car crash. Paris: Dubuffet adapts his new collage style.

1957 New York: Gottlieb begins his *Bursts* series.

1960 New York: De Kooning's *Women* series is resumed.

1962 New York: Kline dies.

1970 New York: Rothko kills himself; Newman dies.

Further Reading

For the New York School, Irving Sandler's *Abstract Expressionism, The Triumph of American Painting*, New York and London, 1970, is the classic and indispensable account. *The New York School, The First Generation*, a catalogue for an exhibition, 'The New York School', 1965, at the Los Angeles County Museum, is an anthology of statements by artists and critics and has been published in book form (London and New York, 1971). Dore Ashton's *The Life and Times of the New York School,* New York and Bath, 1972, is a useful survey of the social, political and cultural background. Clement Greenberg's *Art and Culture,* Boston, 1961, and London, 1973, brings together some of this influential critic's essays, including '"American-Type" Painting'.

Georges Mathieu's *Au-delà du Tachisme,* Paris, 1963, represents the thinking of the artist and publicist most closely associated with Lyrical Abstraction. In *Abstract Art Since 1945,* Brussels, 1970, and London and New York, 1971, there are essays by Werner Haftmann on 'Masters of Gestural Abstraction', Francine C. Legrand on 'The Sign and the "Open" Form' and Michel Ragon on 'Lyrical Abstraction, from Explosion to Inflation'. Books on Dubuffet include *Ecrits de Jean Dubuffet,* Paris, 1967, a collection of his own writings, and *Catalogue des travaux de Jean Dubuffet,* Lausanne, 1966. For the rest the reader must largely apply to exhibition catalogues, such as those of 'Wolfgang Schulze: Wols', Galerie Claude Bernard, Paris, 1958, and 'The Work of Jean Dubuffet', The Museum of Modern Art, New York, 1962.

List of Illustrations

Measurements are given in inches and centimetres, height first.

1 Arshile Gorky (1904–48). *Water of the Flowery Mill,* 1944. Oil on canvas, $42\frac{1}{8} \times 48\frac{3}{4}$ (107.3 × 123.8). Metropolitan Museum of Art, New York. See p. 11.

2 Arshile Gorky (1904–48). *Composition,* 1932–33. Oil on canvas, $48 \times 35\frac{1}{2}$ (122 × 90.5). Private collection. See p. 11.

3 Arshile Gorky (1904–48). *The Betrothal II,* 1947. Oil on canvas, $50\frac{3}{4} \times 38$ (129 × 96.75). Whitney Museum of American Art, New York. See p. 12.

4 Willem De Kooning (1904–). *Pink Angel, c.* 1947. Oil on canvas, 52 × 40 (132 × 106.75). Private collection. See p. 21.

5 Willem De Kooning (1904–). *Seated Woman, c.* 1940. Oil on canvas, 54 × 36 (137.25 × 91.25). Private collection. See p. 21.

6 Willem De Kooning (1904–). *Excavation,* 1950. Oil on canvas, $80\frac{1}{8} \times 100\frac{1}{8}$ (204.4 × 254.25). Courtesy of The Art Institute of Chicago. See p. 24.

7 Willem De Kooning (1904–). *Door to the River*, 1960. Oil on canvas, $78 \times 69\frac{7}{8}$ (203.2 × 177.8). Whitney Museum of American Art, New York. See p. 24.

8 Jackson Pollock (1912–56). *The She-Wolf*, 1943. Oil, gouache, and plaster on canvas, $41\frac{7}{8} \times 67$ (106.7 × 170.2). The Museum of Modern Art, New York. Purchase. See pp. 17–18.

9 Jackson Pollock (1912–56). *The Flame*, 1937. Oil on canvas, $20\frac{1}{8} \times 30\frac{1}{8}$ (51.2 × 76.4). Collection Lee Krasner Pollock; courtesy of Marlborough Gallery, Inc., New York. See p. 16.

10 Jackson Pollock (1912–56). *Blue Poles*, 1953. Oil, Duco and aluminium paint on canvas, $83 \times 192\frac{1}{2}$ (210.8 × 488.9). Private collection. See p. 18.

11 Jackson Pollock (1912–56). *One (No. 31)*, 1950. Oil and enamel on canvas, $106 \times 209\frac{5}{8}$ (269.25 × 532.5). Collection, The Museum of Modern Art, New York. Gift of Sidney Janis. See p. 18.

12 Jackson Pollock (1912–56). *Cathedral*, 1947. Duco and aluminium paint on canvas, 71 × 35 (180.3 × 89). Dallas Museum of Fine Arts, Texas. See p. 18.

13 Jackson Pollock (1912–56). *Easter and the Totem*, 1953. Oil on canvas, $82\frac{1}{8} \times 57\frac{7}{8}$ (208.6 × 147.3). Collection Lee Krasner Pollock; courtesy of Marlborough Gallery, Inc., New York. See p. 20.

14 Mark Tobey (1890–). *Edge of August*, 1953. Casein on composition board, 48 × 28 (122 × 71). Collection, The Museum of Modern Art, New York. Purchase. See p. 14.

15 Mark Rothko (1903–70). *Entombment I*, 1946. Oil on canvas, $20\frac{3}{8} \times 25\frac{3}{4}$ (51.8 × 65.4). Whitney Museum of American Art, New York. See p. 28.

16 Mark Rothko (1903–70). *Black on Grey*, 1970. Acrylic on canvas, 68 × 64 (173 × 162.5). Estate of Mark Rothko; courtesy of Marlborough Gallery, Inc., New York. See p. 29.

17 Mark Rothko (1903–70). *Red, White and Brown*, 1957. Oil on canvas, $99\frac{1}{2} \times 81\frac{3}{4}$ (252.8 × 207.8). Kunstmuseum, Basle. See p. 29.

18 Adolph Gottlieb (1903–74). *The Frozen Sounds Number 1*, 1951. Oil on canvas, 36 × 48 (91.4 × 122). Whitney Museum of American Art, New York. Gift of Mr and Mrs Samuel Kootz. See pp. 29–30.

19 Adolph Gottlieb (1903–74). *Brink*, 1959. Acrylic on canvas, 90 × 108 (228.8 × 274.4). Private collection. See p. 30.

20 Hans Hofmann (1880–1966). *Transfiguration*, 1947. Oil on canvas, 60 × 48 (152.4 × 132.1). André Emmerich Gallery, New York. See p. 33.

21 Hans Hofmann (1880–1966). *Rising Moon*, 1964. Oil on canvas, 84 × 78 (213.4 × 198). André Emmerich Gallery, New York. See p. 34.

22 Hans Hofmann (1880–1966). *Fantasia in Blue*, 1954. Oil on canvas, 60 × 48 (152.4 × 132.1). Whitney Museum of American Art, New York. See p. 34.

23 William Baziotes (1912–63). *Dwarf*, 1947. Oil on canvas, 42 × 36⅛ (106.5 × 91.75). Collection, The Museum of Modern Art, New York; A. Conger Goodyear Fund. See p. 13.

24 Franz Kline (1910–62). *King Oliver*, 1958. Oil on canvas, 99 × 77½ (251.4 × 196.8). Private collection. See pp. 37, 50.

25 Robert Motherwell (1915–). *Je t'aime, II A*, 1955. Oil on canvas, 72 × 54 (183 × 137.4). Private collection. See p. 34.

26 Robert Motherwell (1915–). *Elegy to the Spanish Republic*, 1953–54. Oil on canvas, 80 × 100 (203.4 × 254). Albright-Knox Art Gallery, Buffalo, New York. Gift of Seymour H. Knox. See p. 34.

27 Clyfford Still (1904–). *Painting 1948–D*, 1948. Oil on canvas, 93 × 79⅜ (236.5 × 202.2). Private collection. See p. 31.

28 Clyfford Still (1904–). *1951 Yellow*, 1951. Oil on canvas, 109½ × 92¼ (278 × 229.5). Private collection. See p. 31.

29 Clyfford Still (1904–). *Painting 1958*. Oil on canvas, 113¾ × 159½ (288.9 × 405.1). Private collection. See p. 31.

30 Clyfford Still (1904–). *Painting 1951*. Oil on canvas, 93¼ × 75¾ (238 × 192.25). The Detroit Institute of Art, Detroit, Michigan. See p. 31.

31 Barnett Newman (1905–70). *Untitled*, 1945. Oil on canvas, 36 × 24¼ (91 × 62). Estate of the Artist. See p. 27.

32 Barnett Newman (1905–70). *Onement I*, 1948. Oil on canvas, 27 × 16 (69 × 41). Collection Annalee Newman. See p. 27.

33 Barnett Newman (1905–70). *Vir Heroicus Sublimis*, 1950–51. Oil on canvas, 95⅜ × 213¼ (242.4 × 541). The Museum of Modern Art, New York. Gift of Mr and Mrs Ben Heller. See p. 27.

34 Barnett Newman (1905–70). *Achilles*, 1952. Oil on canvas, 96 × 79 (244 × 201). Collection Annalee Newman. See p. 27.

35 Ad Reinhardt (1913–). *Painting*, 1950. Oil on canvas, 30½ × 40½ (77.5 × 103). See p. 32.

36 Ad Reinhardt (1913–). *Red Painting*, 1952. Oil on canvas, 144 × 76 (365.9 × 193). The Metropolitan Museum of Art, New York. Arthur H. Hearn Fund, 1968. See p. 32.

37 Morris Louis (1912–62). *Untitled*, 1959. Magna acrylic on canvas, 104 × 76 (269.5 × 193). Photo Kasmin Gallery, London. See p. 40.

38 Morris Louis (1912–62). *Sky Gamut*, 1961. Acrylic on canvas, 90½ × 56¼ (230 × 143). Private collection. See p. 40.

39 Bradley Walker Tomlin (1899–1953). *No. 20*, 1949. Oil on canvas, 86 × 80¼ (219.5 × 204). Collection, The Museum of Modern Art, New York. Gift of Philip Johnson. See p. 39.

40 James Brooks (1906–). *Number 36*, 1950. Oil on bemis cloth, 41 × 45 (104 × 114.5). Collection the artist. See p. 39.

41 Philip Guston (1913–). *Passage*, 1957–58. Oil on canvas, 65 × 74 (165.1 × 188). Private collection. See p. 38.

42 Helen Frankenthaler (1928–). *Blue Territory*, 1955. Oil on canvas, 113 × 58 (287 × 147.3). Whitney Museum of American Art, New York. See p. 40.

43 Jean Fautrier (1897–). *Hostage*, 1945. Oil on canvas, 10¾ × 8½ (27.25 × 21.75). Private collection, London. See p. 47.

44 Wols (Alfred Otto Wolfgang Schulze) (1913–51). *Composition V*, 1946. 6⅛ × 4⅞ (15.9 × 12.3). Musée National d'Art Moderne, Paris. See p. 43.

45 Jean Dubuffet (1901–). *Table, Constant Companion*, 1953. Oil on canvas, 38 × 50¾ (96.5 × 129). Moderna Museet, Stockholm. See p. 45.

46 Jean-Paul Riopelle (1924–). *Painting*, 1951–52. Oil on

canvas, $44\frac{7}{8} \times 76\frac{3}{4}$ (114 × 195). Galerie Stadler, Paris. See p. 48.

47 Hans Hartung (1904–), *T 1958–4*, 1958. Oil on canvas, $36\frac{1}{4} \times 23\frac{5}{8}$ (92 × 60). Saidenberg Gallery, New York. See p. 50.

48 Pierre Soulages (1919–). *Painting*, 1959. Oil on canvas, $63\frac{3}{4} \times 44\frac{7}{8}$ (162 × 114). Collection the artist, Paris. See p. 50.

49 Alberto Burri (1915–). *Sack No. 5*, 1953. Collage, $59\frac{1}{8} \times 51\frac{1}{4}$ (150.25 × 130.25). Collection the artist. See p. 47.

50 Antoni Tàpies (1928–). *White and Orange*, 1967. Mixed media on plywood, $19\frac{5}{8} \times 24$ (50 × 61). Collection Teresa B. de Tàpies, Barcelona. See p. 45.

51 Jean Bazaine (1904–). *Child and the Night*, 1949. Oil on canvas, $36\frac{1}{4} \times 28\frac{3}{4}$ (95 × 73). Private collection. See p. 52.

52 Alfred Manessier (1911–). *Night in Gethsemane*, 1952. Oil on canvas, 78 × $58\frac{1}{4}$ (198 × 148). Kunstsammlung Nordrhein-Westfalen, Düsseldorf. See p. 52.

53 Asger Jorn (1914–). *Unlimited*, 1959–60. Oil on canvas, $18\frac{1}{8} \times 21\frac{5}{8}$ (46 × 55). See p. 54.

54 Alan Davie (1920–). *Heavenly Bridge No. 3*, 1960. Oil on canvas, $39\frac{3}{4} \times 48$ (101 × 122). Gimpel Fils, London. See p. 56.

55 Karel Appel (1921–). *Two Heads in a Landscape*, 1958. Oil on canvas, 35 × $45\frac{5}{8}$ (89 × 116). Private collection. See p. 55.

56 Maurice Estève (1904–). *Friselune*, 1958. Oil on canvas. Nasjonalgalleriet, Oslo. See p. 52.

57 Nicolas de Staël (1914–55). *Figure Beside the Sea*, 1952. Oil on canvas, $63\frac{3}{4} \times 51\frac{1}{4}$ (167 × 130.25). Kunstsammlung Nordrhein-Westfalen, Düsseldorf. See p. 52.

58 Patrick Heron (1920–). *Manganese in Deep Violet: January 1967*, 1967. Oil on canvas, 40 × 60 (101.75 × 52.25). Private collection. See p. 56.

59 Corneille (Cornelis van Beverloo, 1922–). *Play of Sun on Waves*, 1958. Oil on canvas, $51\frac{1}{4} \times 35$ (130 × 89). Collection Haags Gemeentemuseum, The Hague. See pp. 54–55.

60 Georges Mathieu (1922–). *Mathieu from Alsace goes to Ramsey Abbey*. Oil on canvas. Collection Anthony Denney, London. See p. 51.

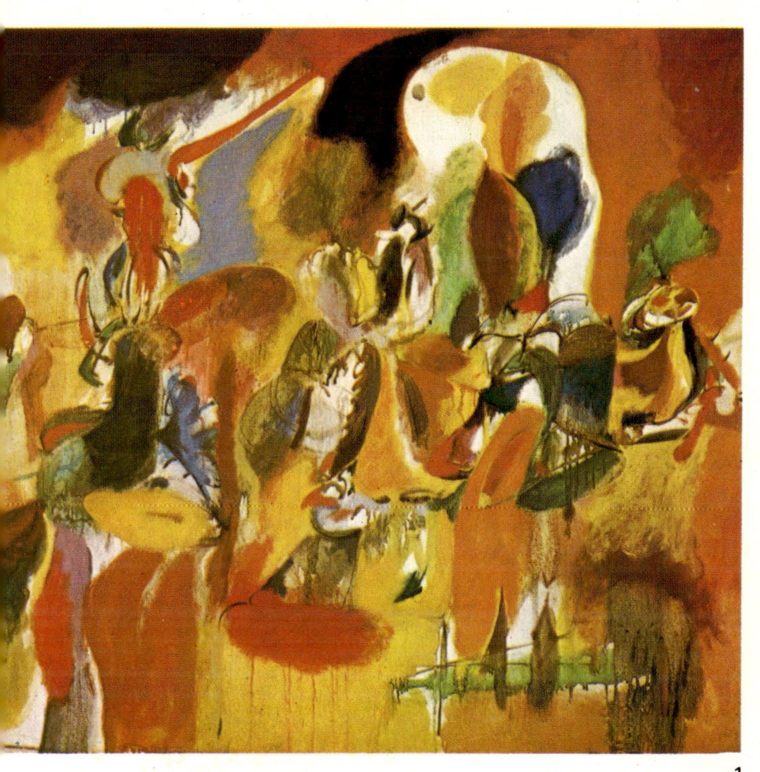

1

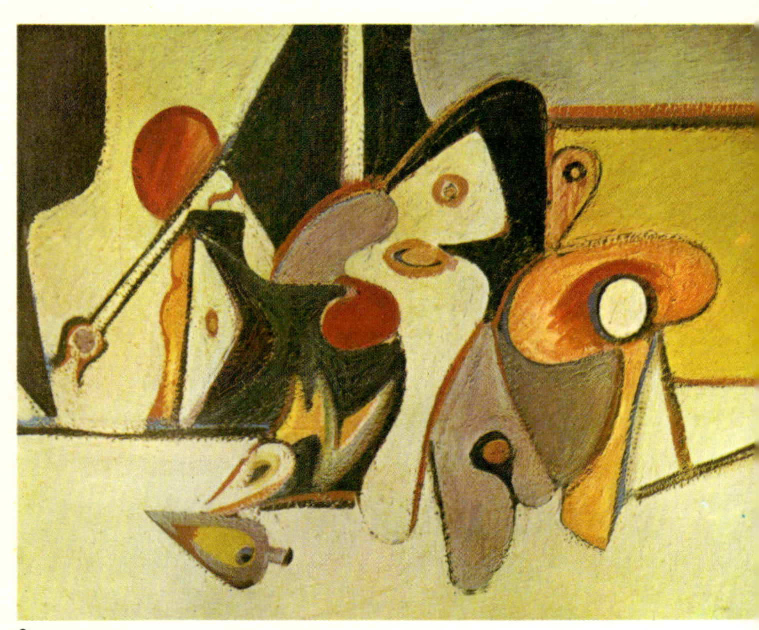

2

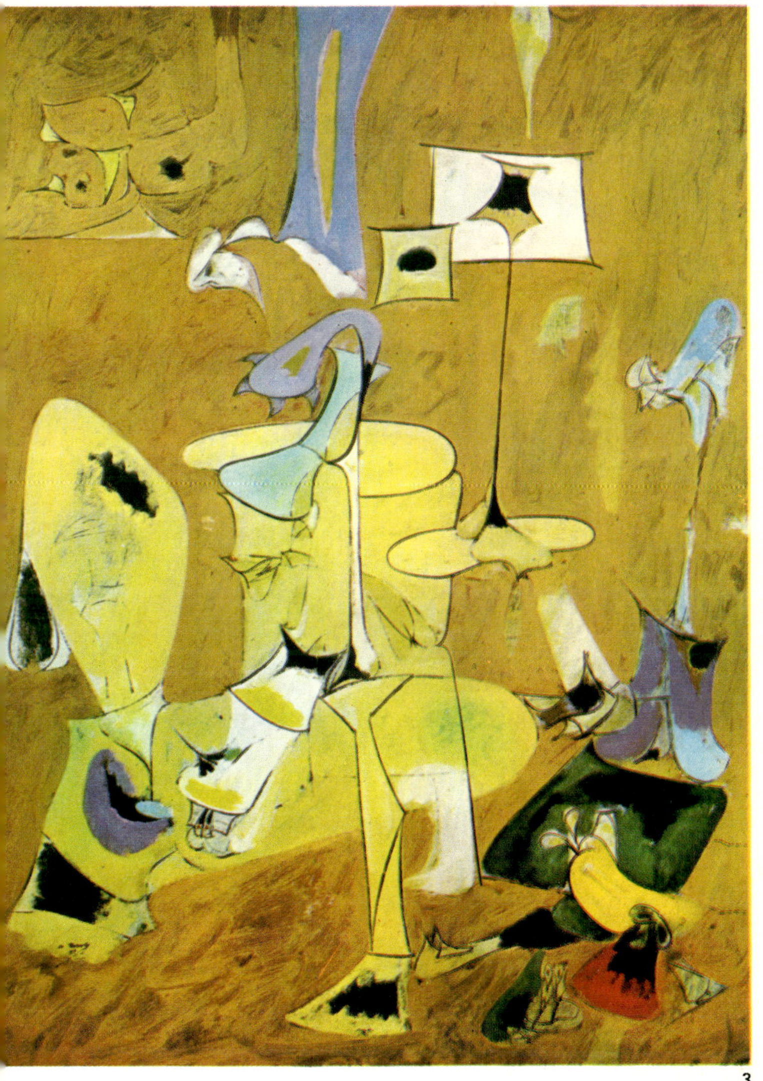

3

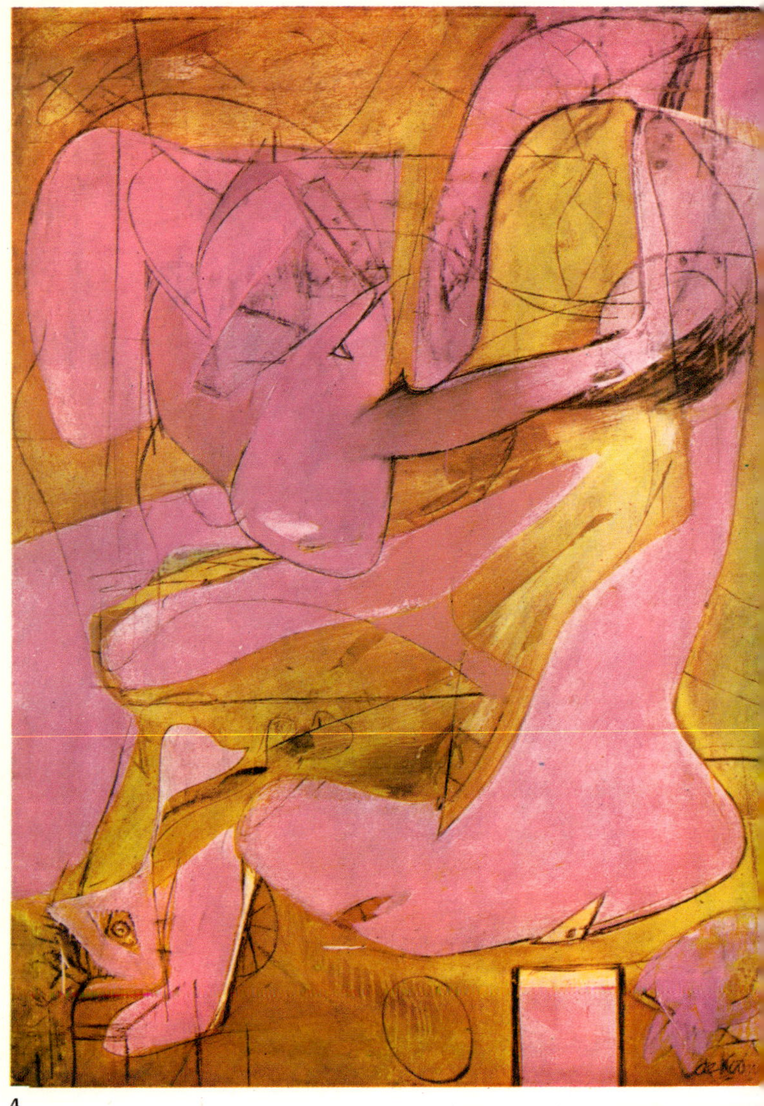

4

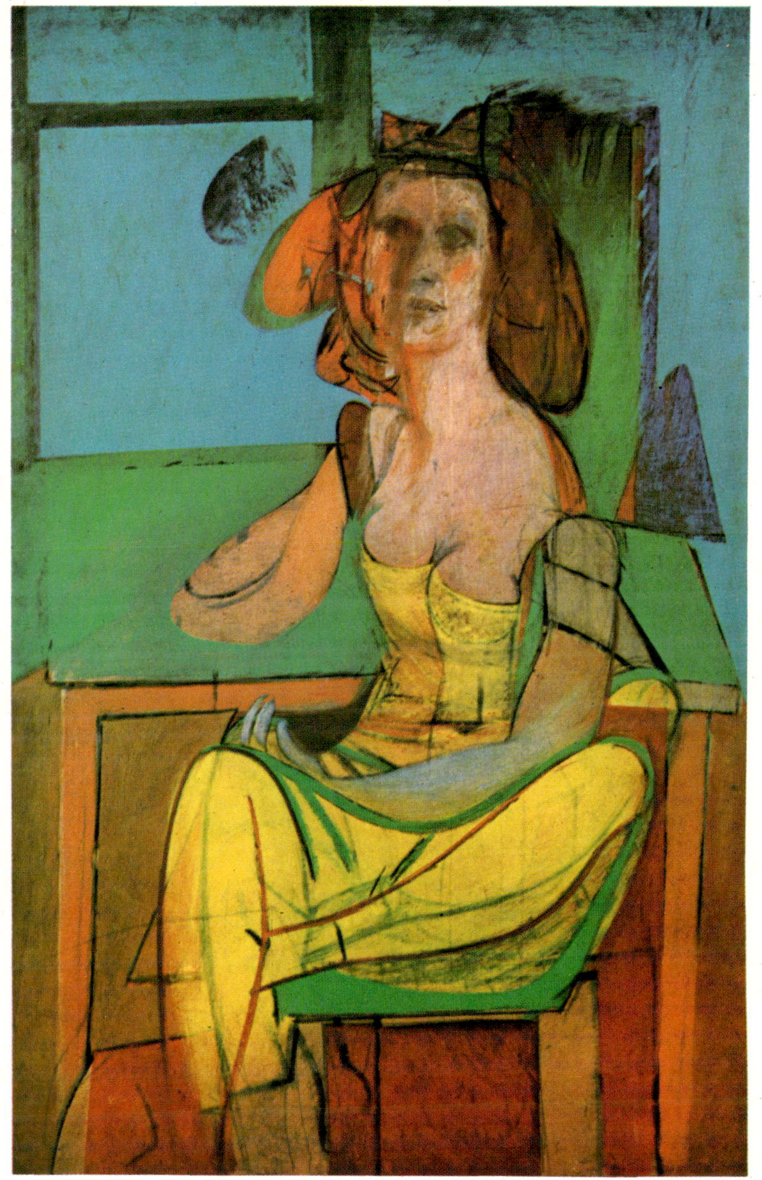

5

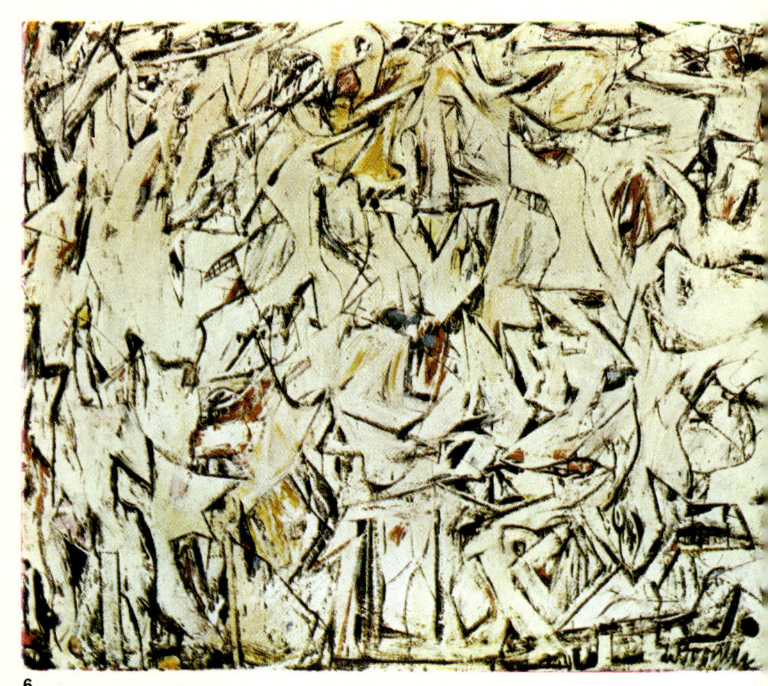

6

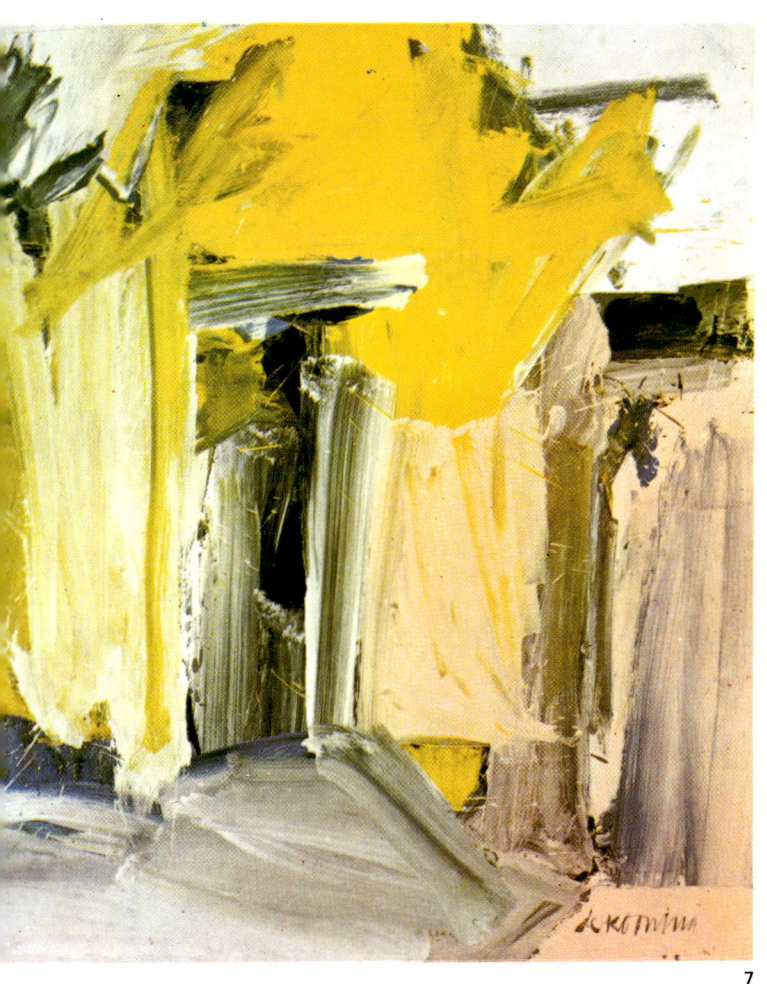

7

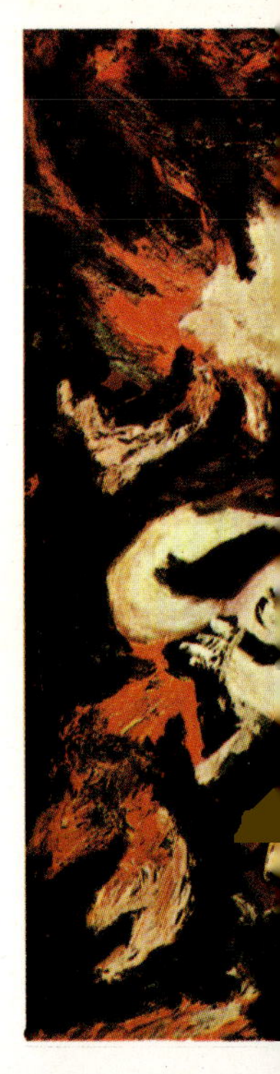

8

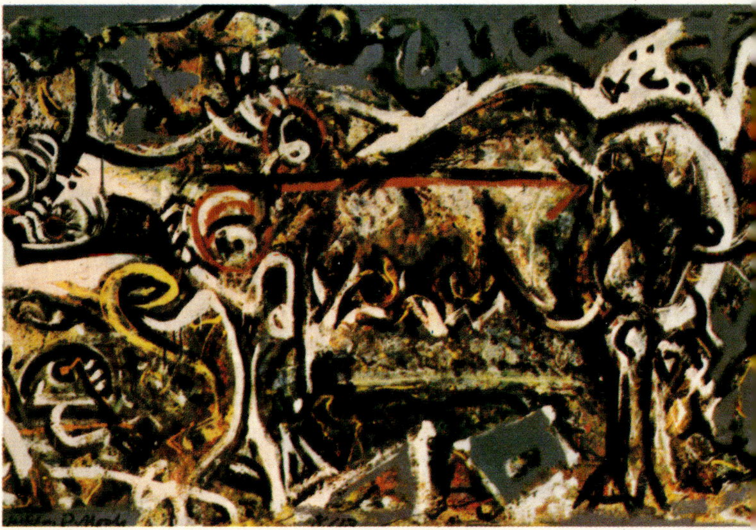

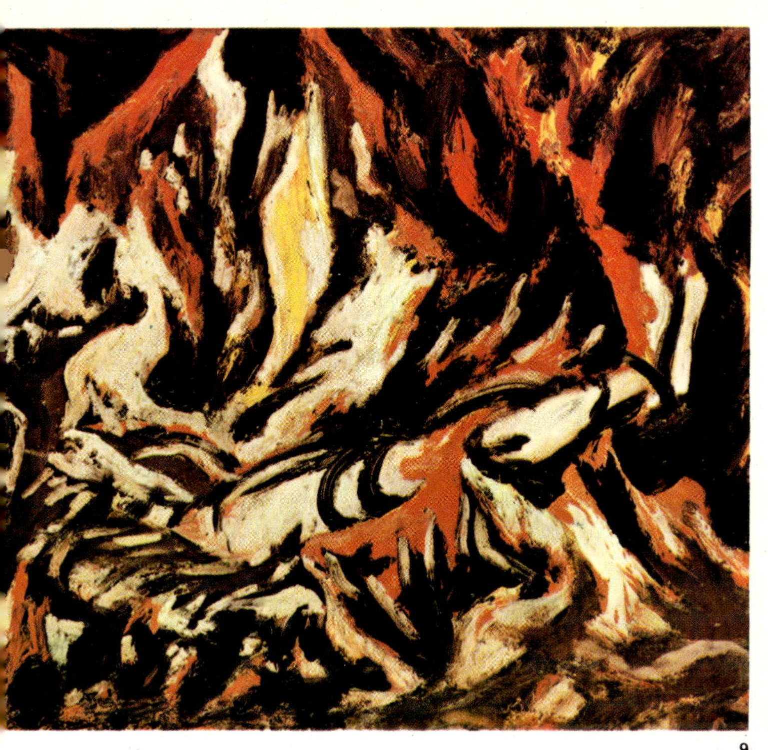

9

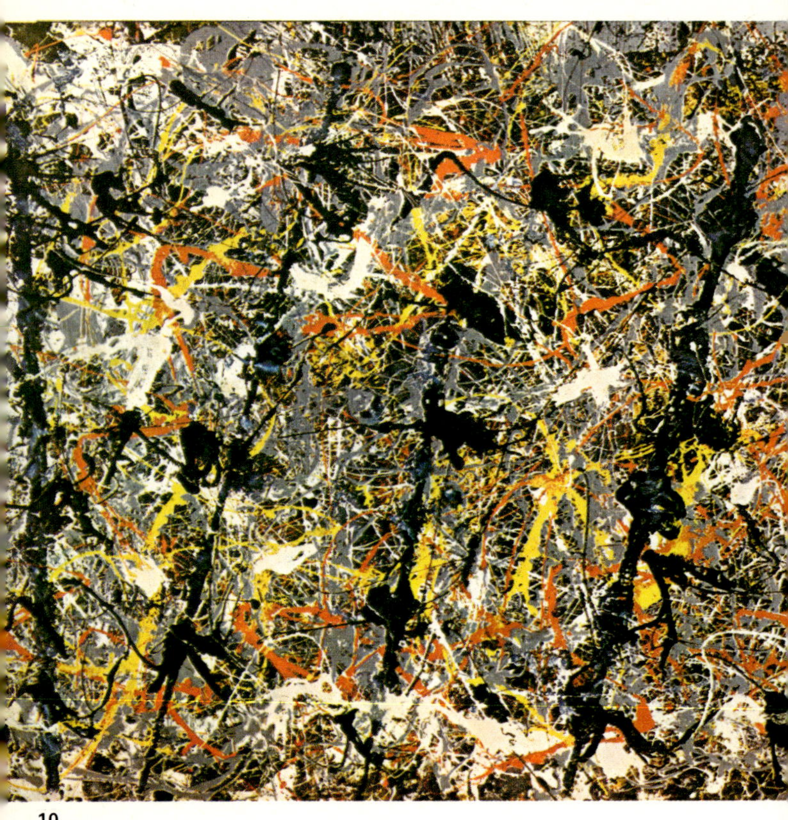

10

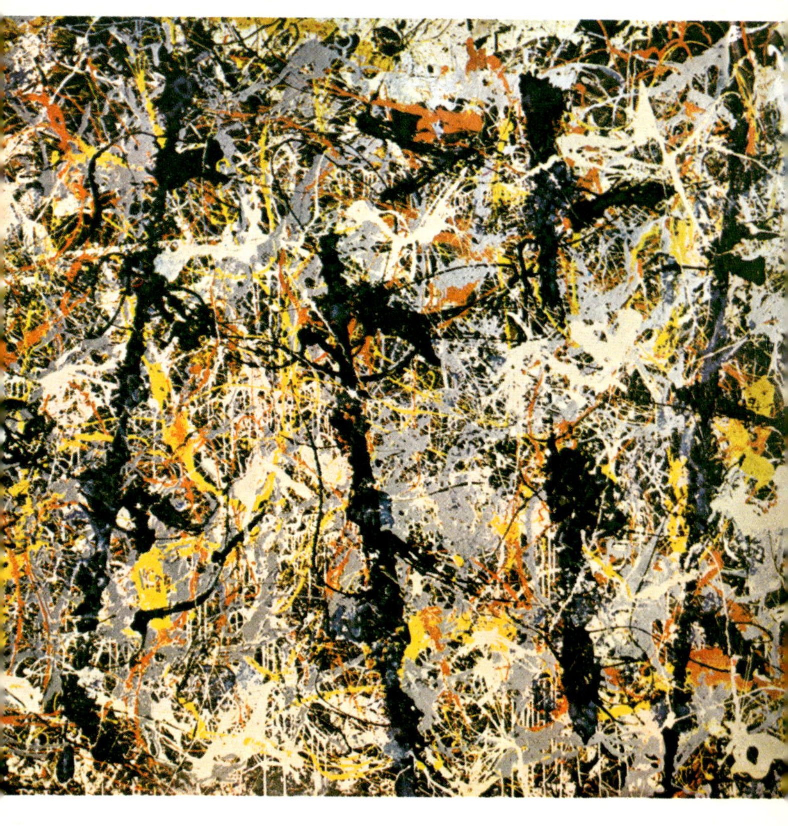

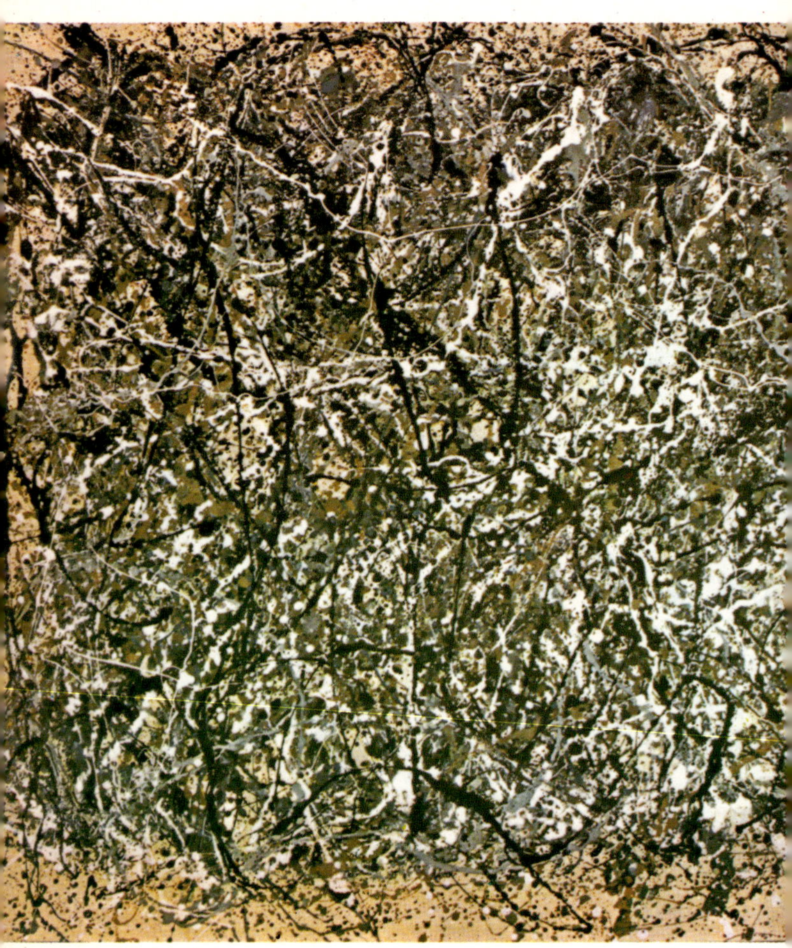

11

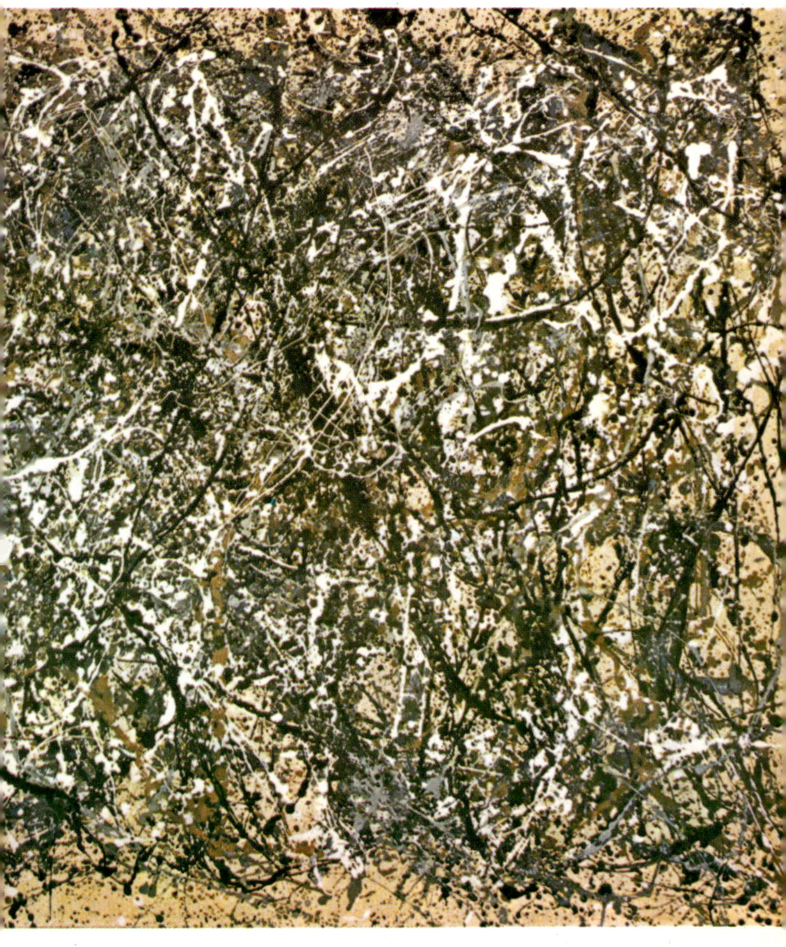

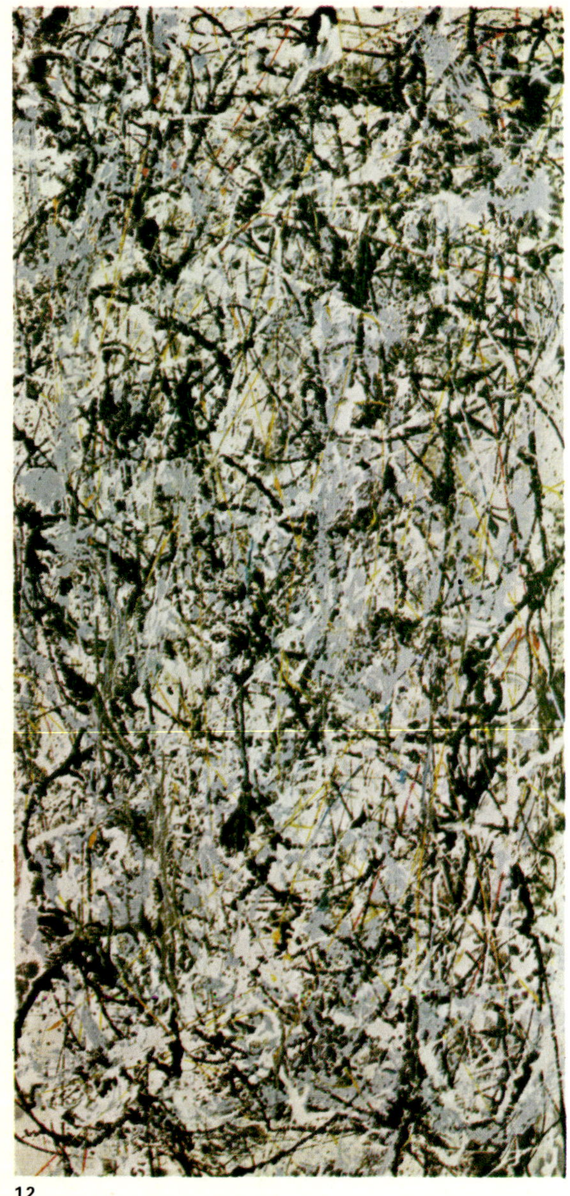

12

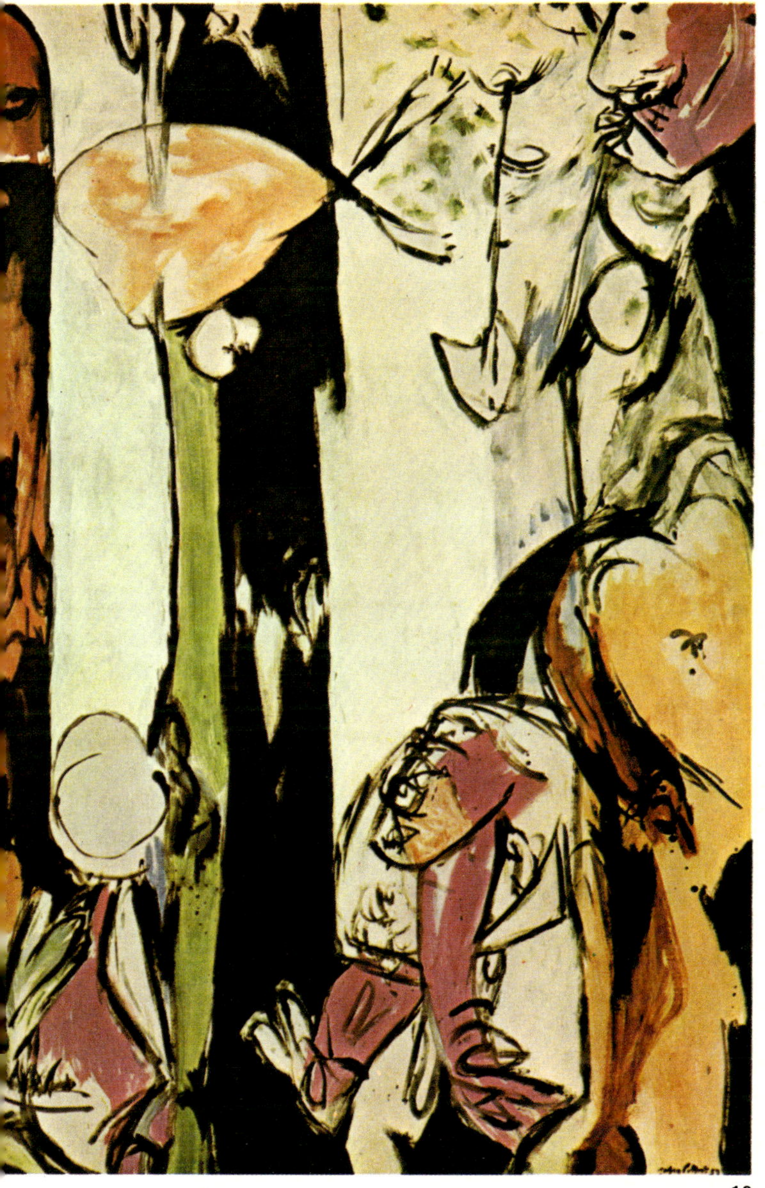

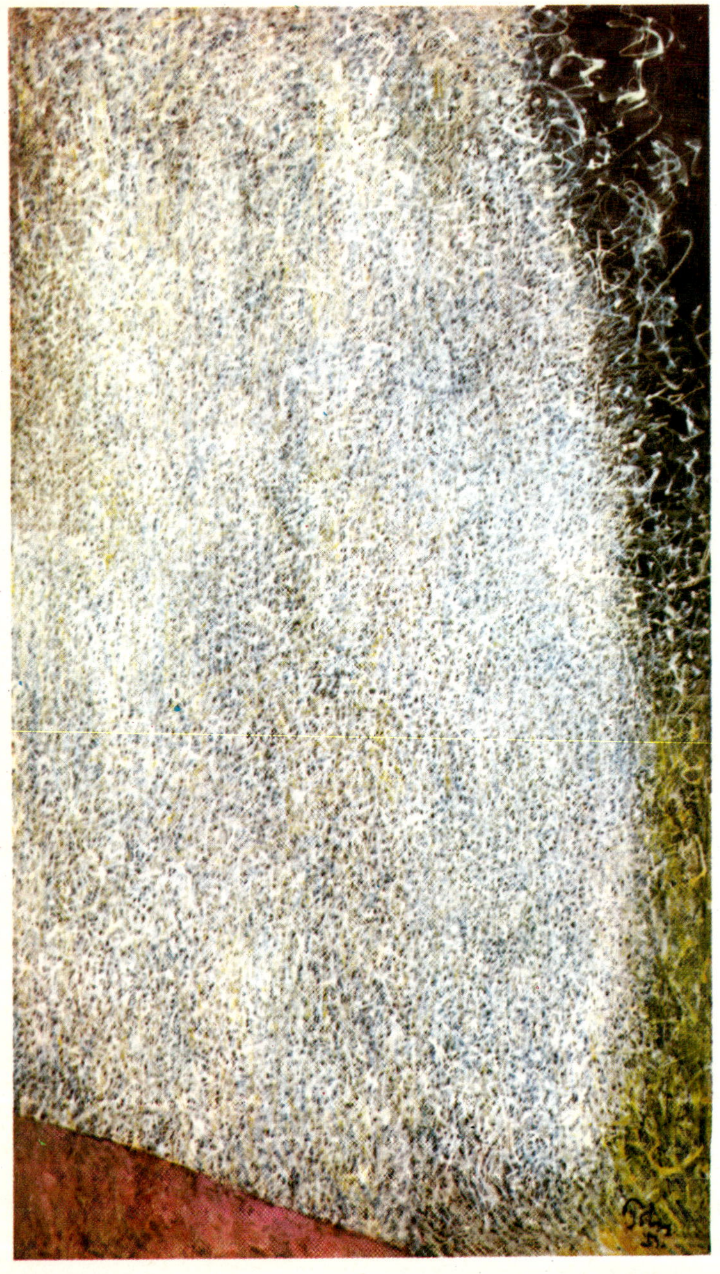

14

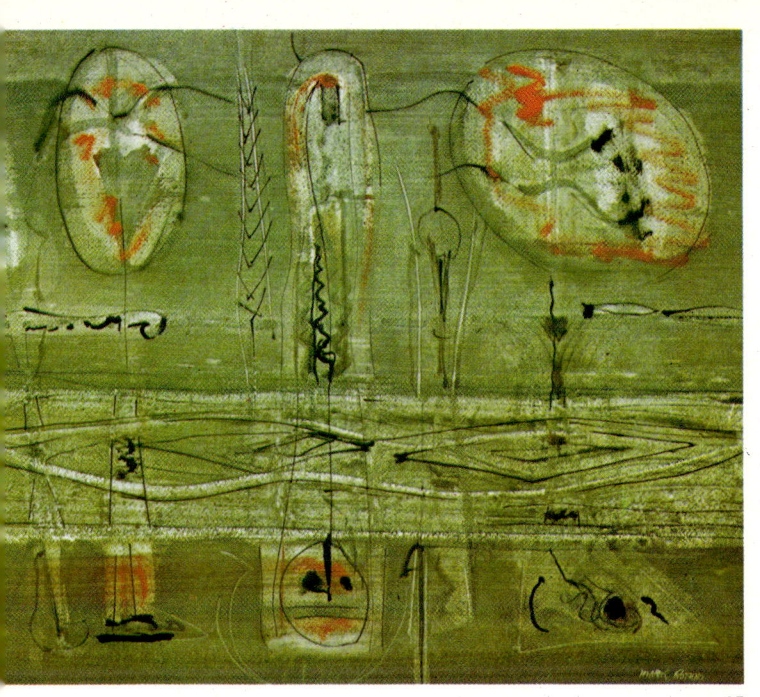

15

16

17

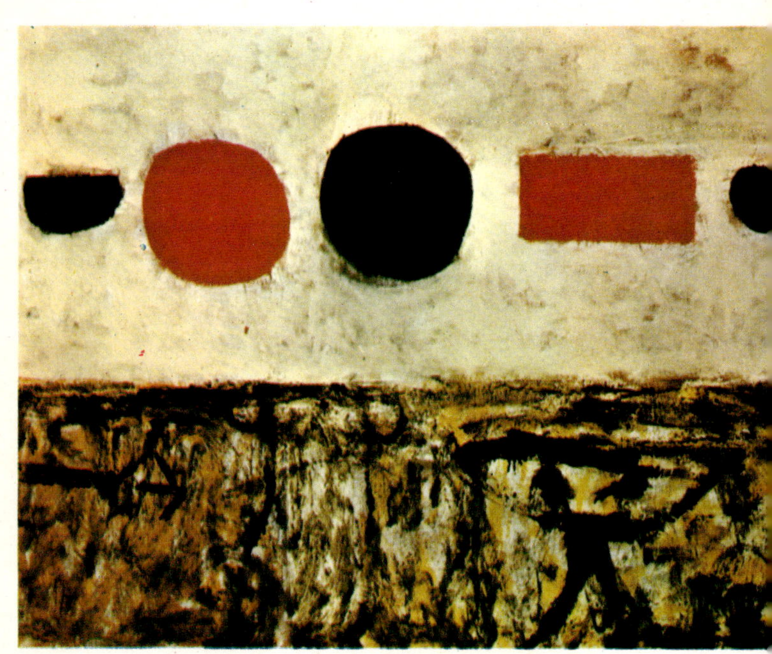

18

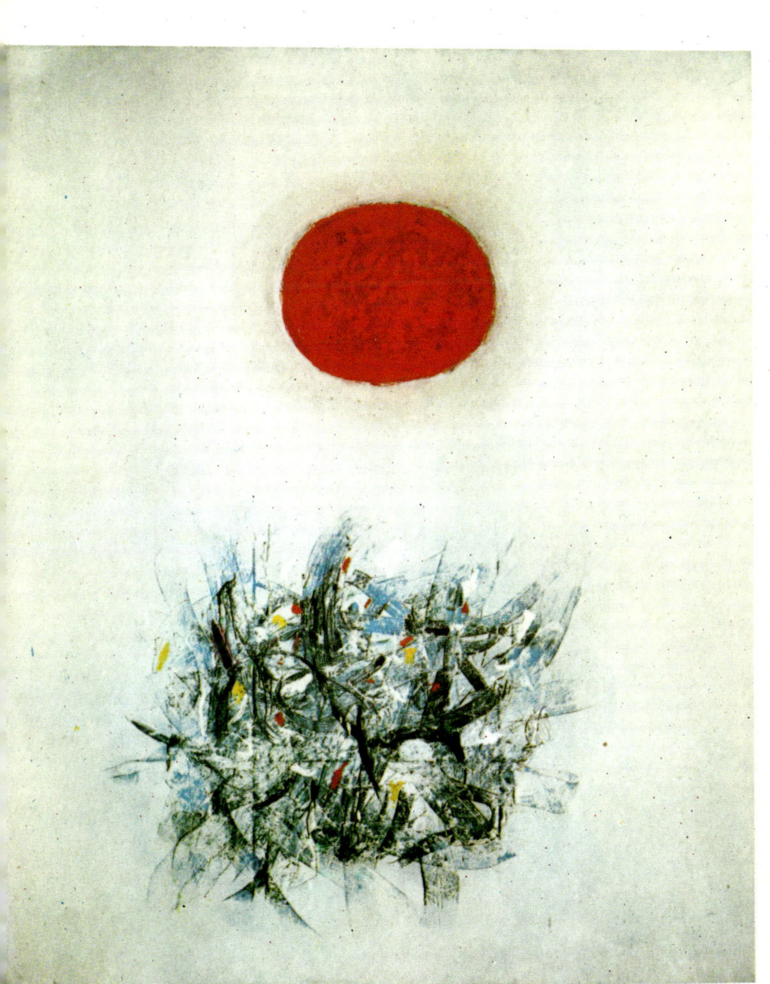

19

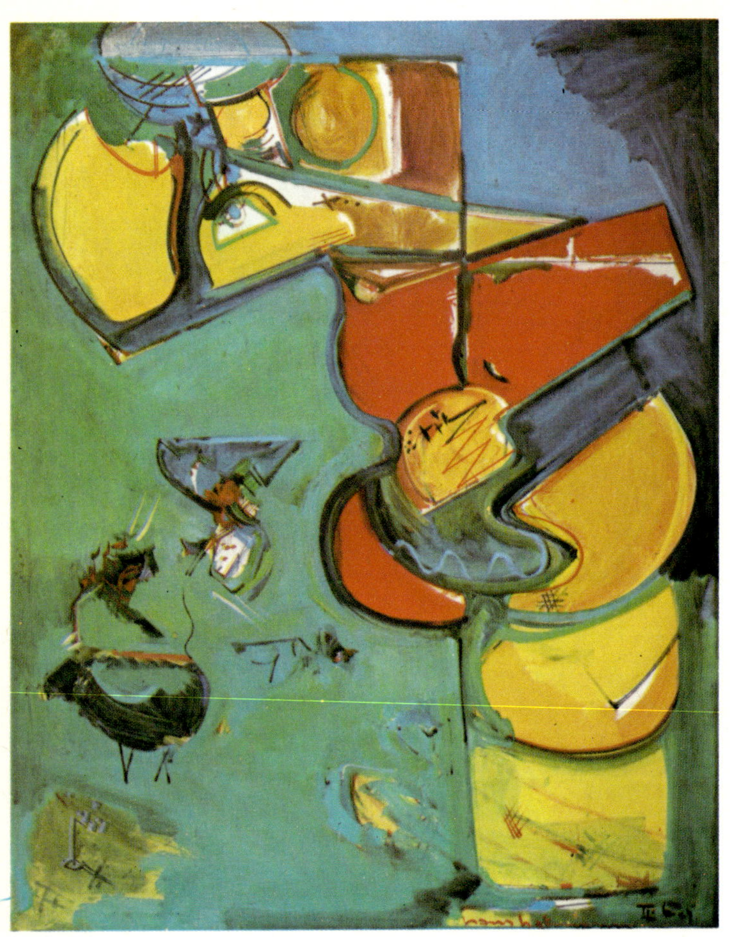

20

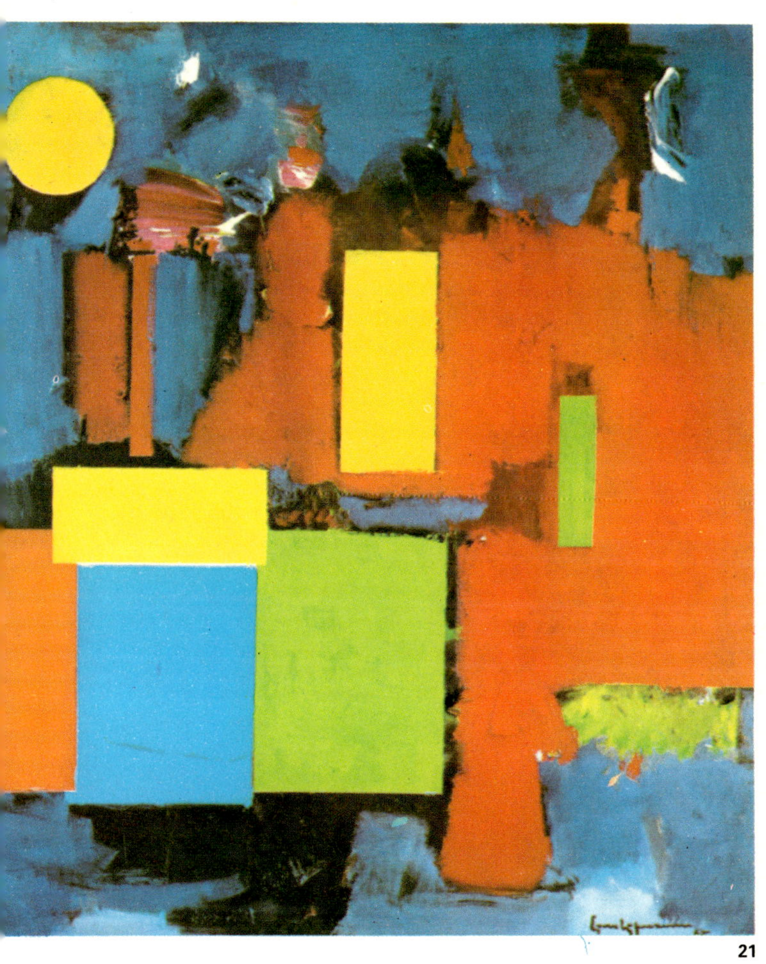

21

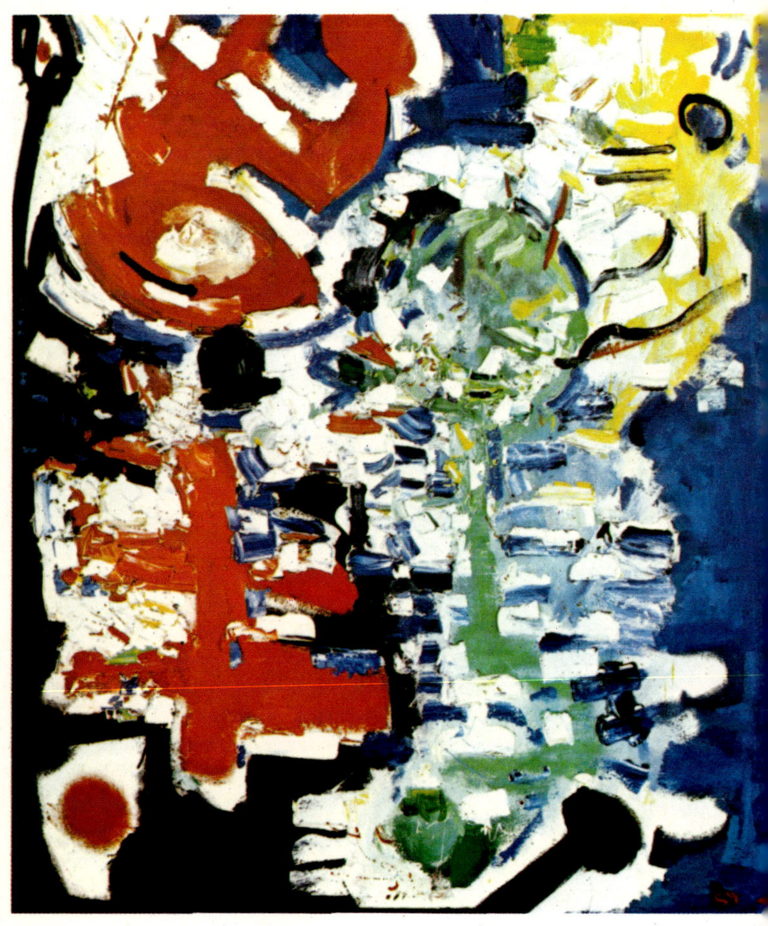

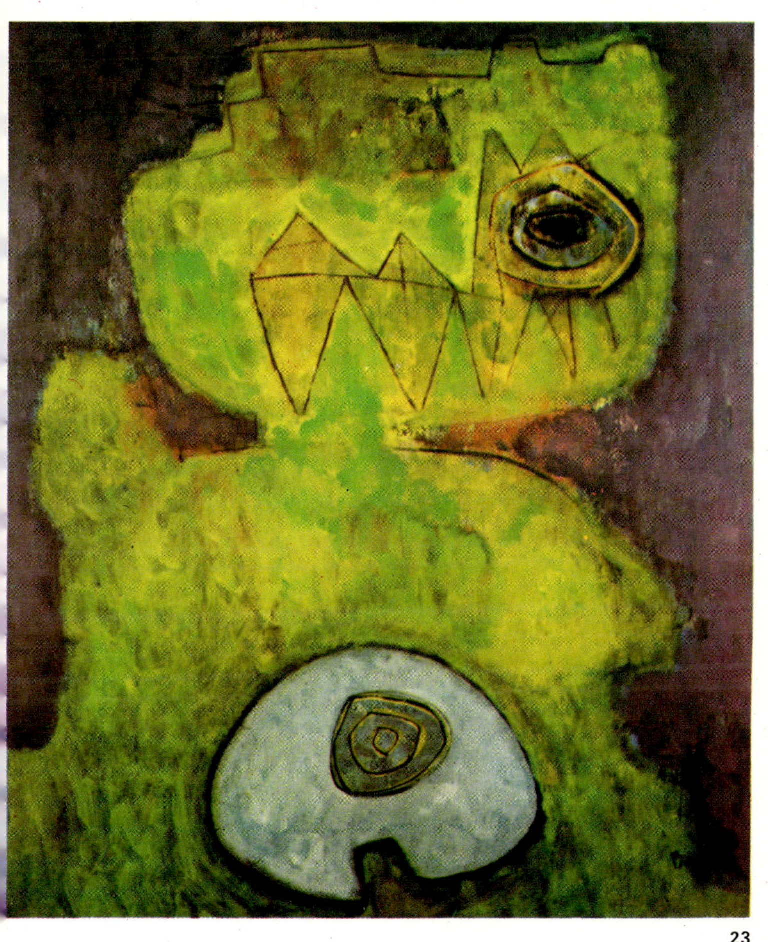

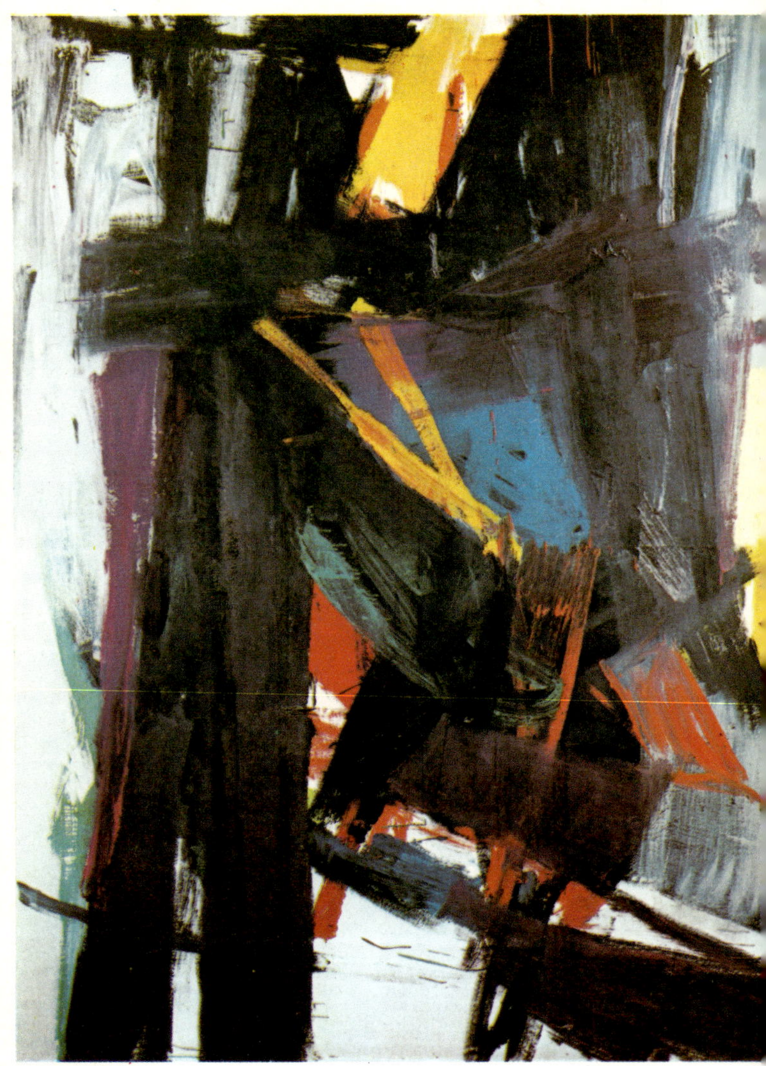

24

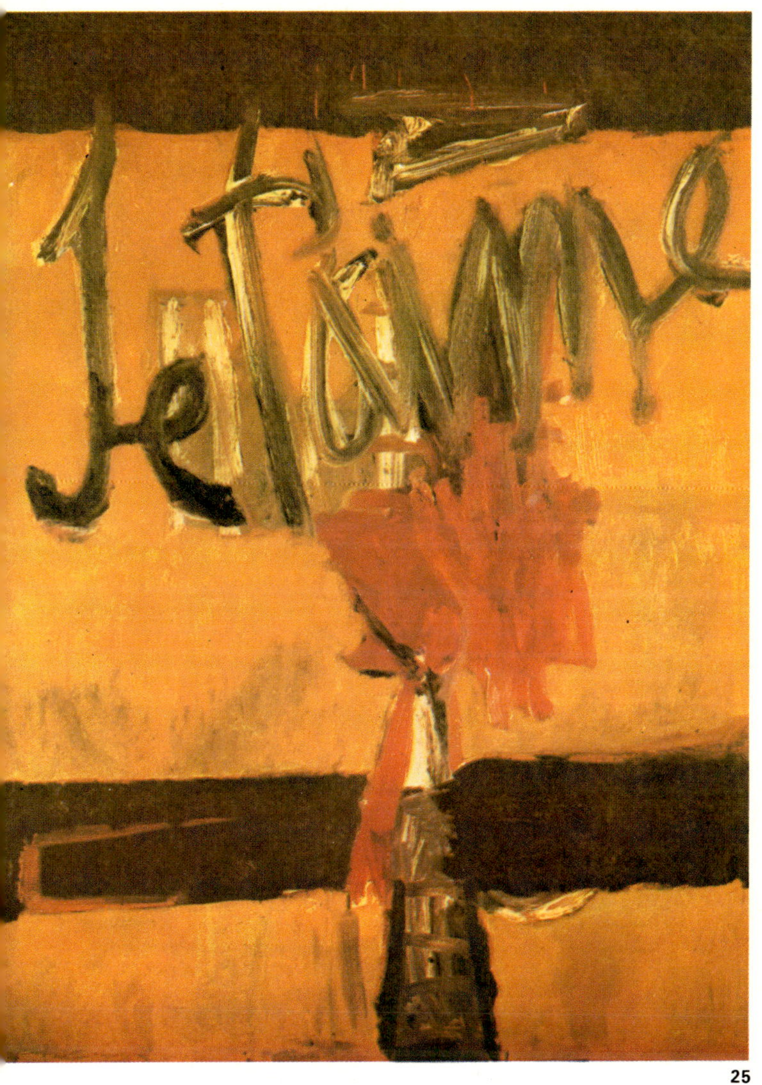

25

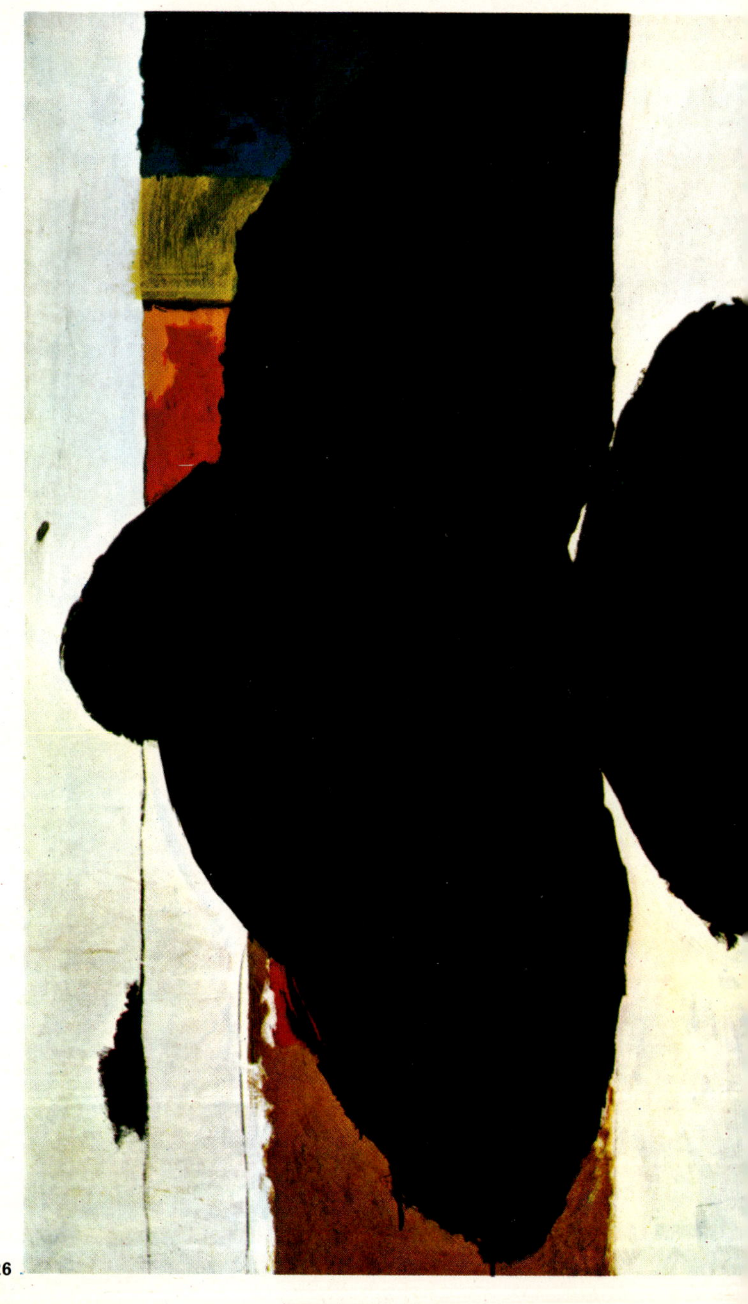

27

28

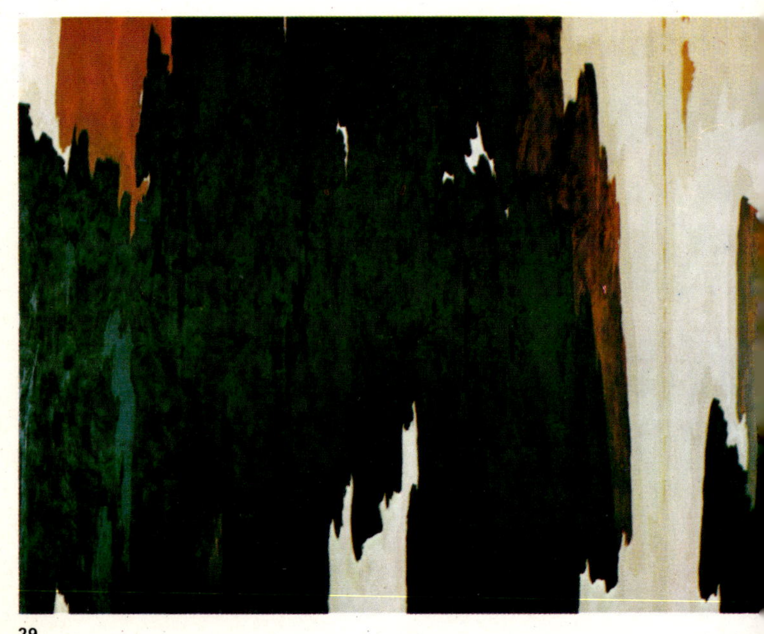

29

30

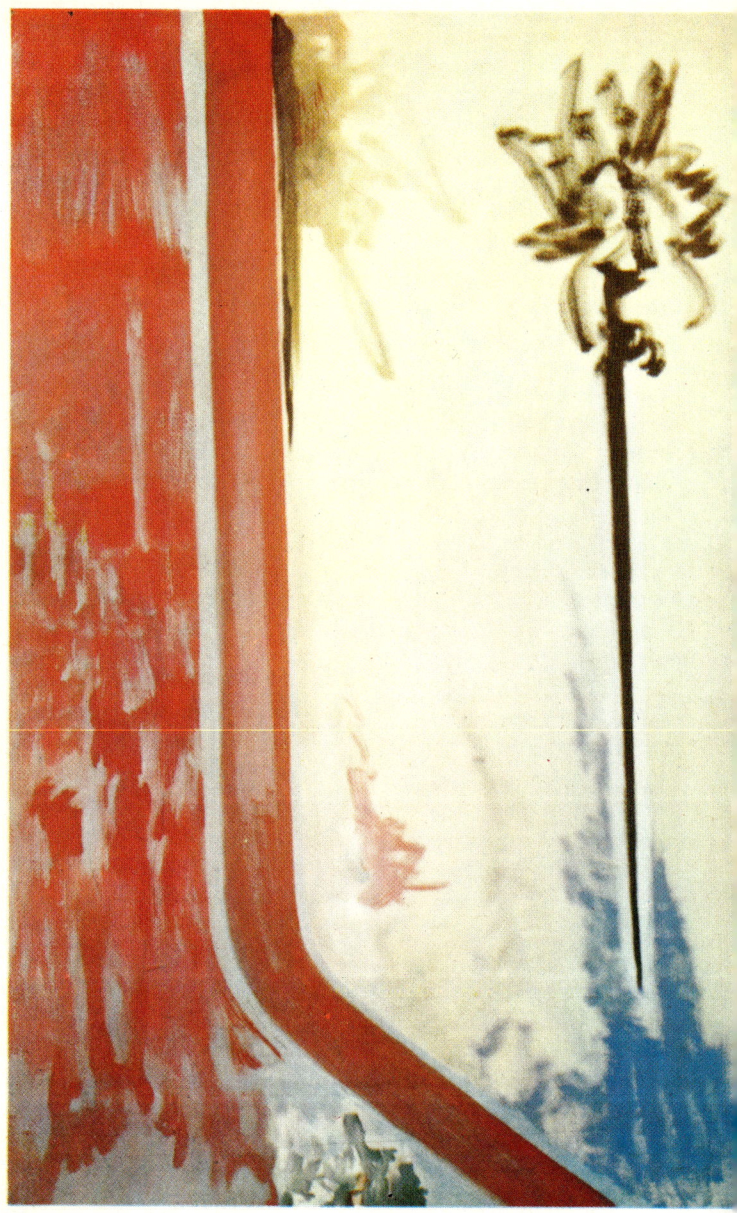

31

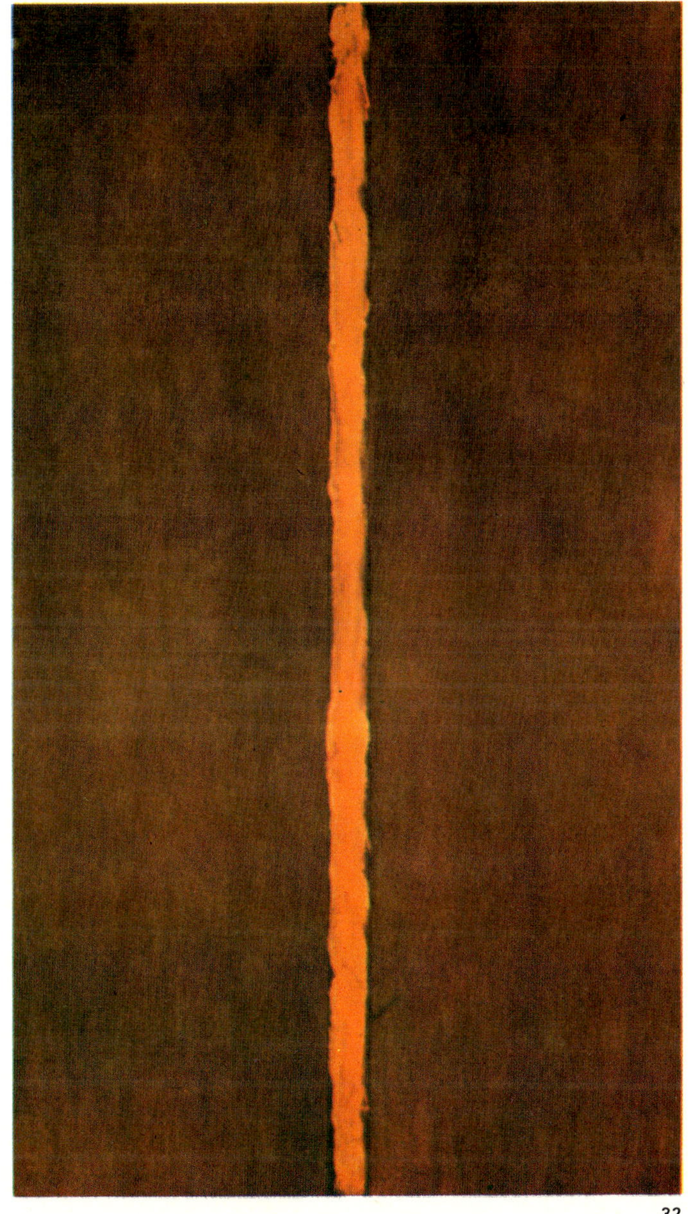

32

34

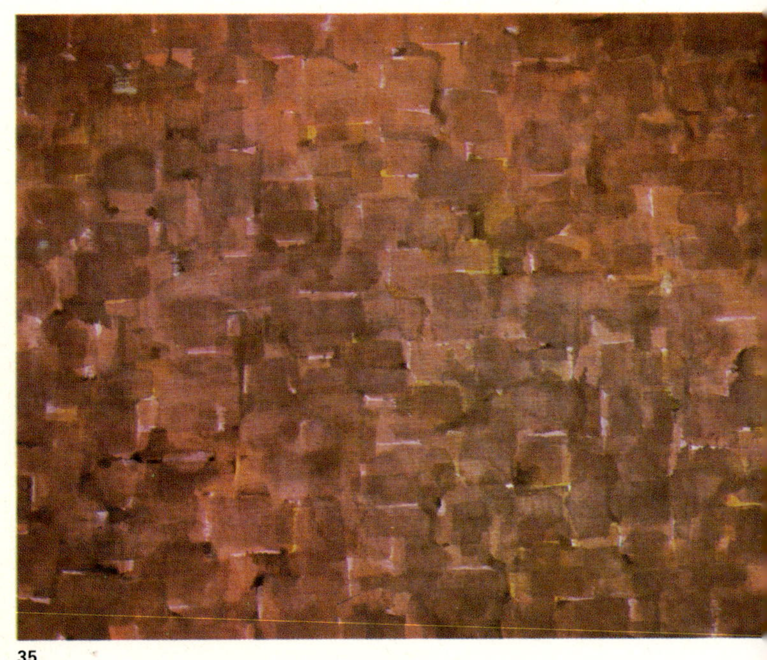

35

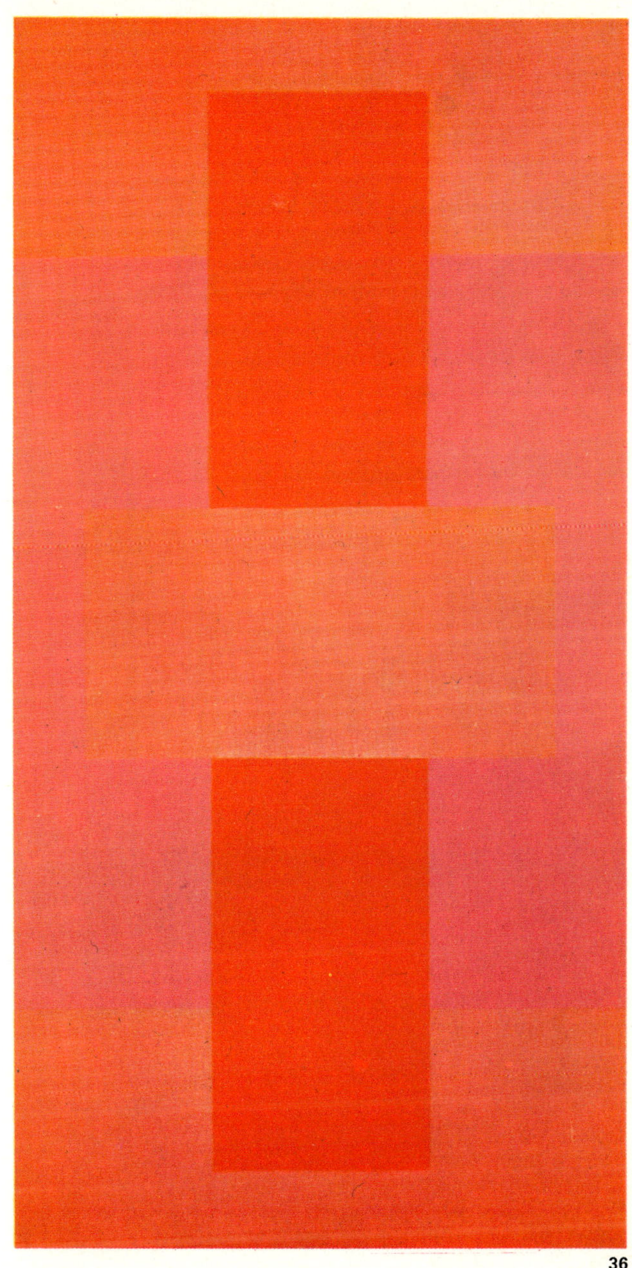

36

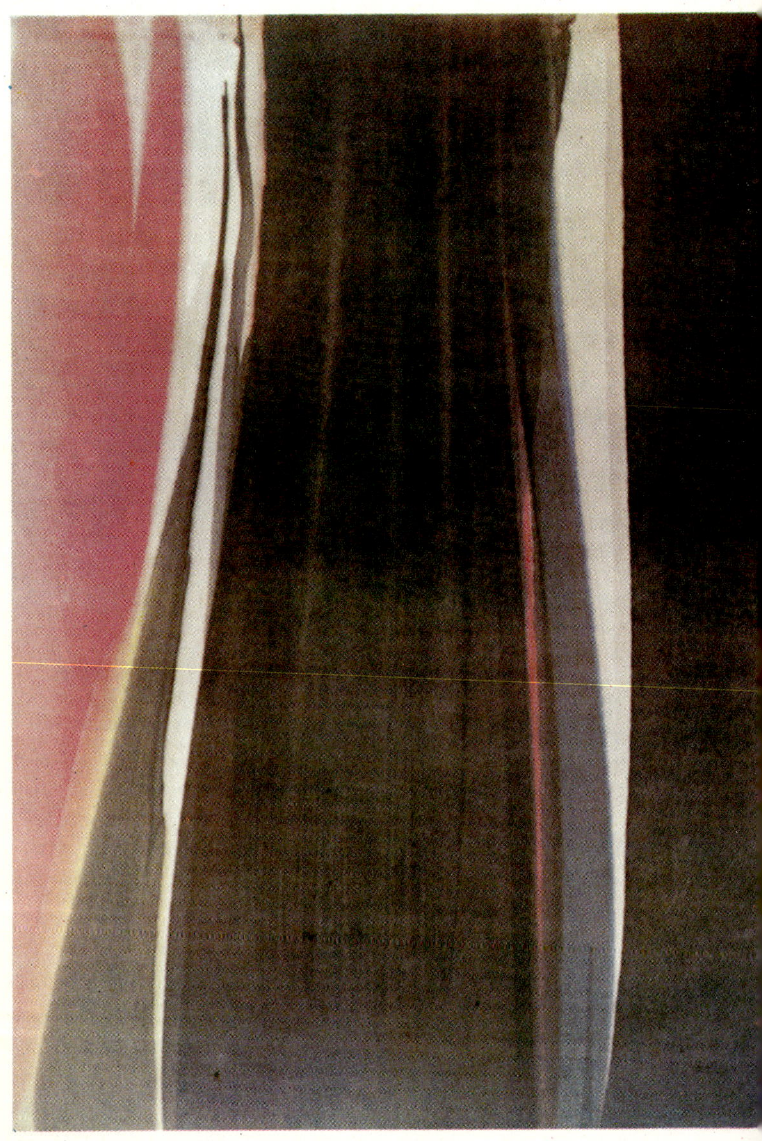

37

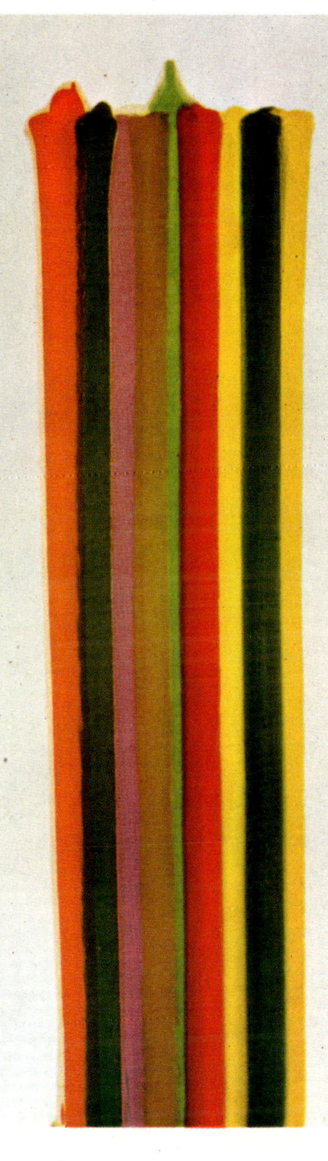

38

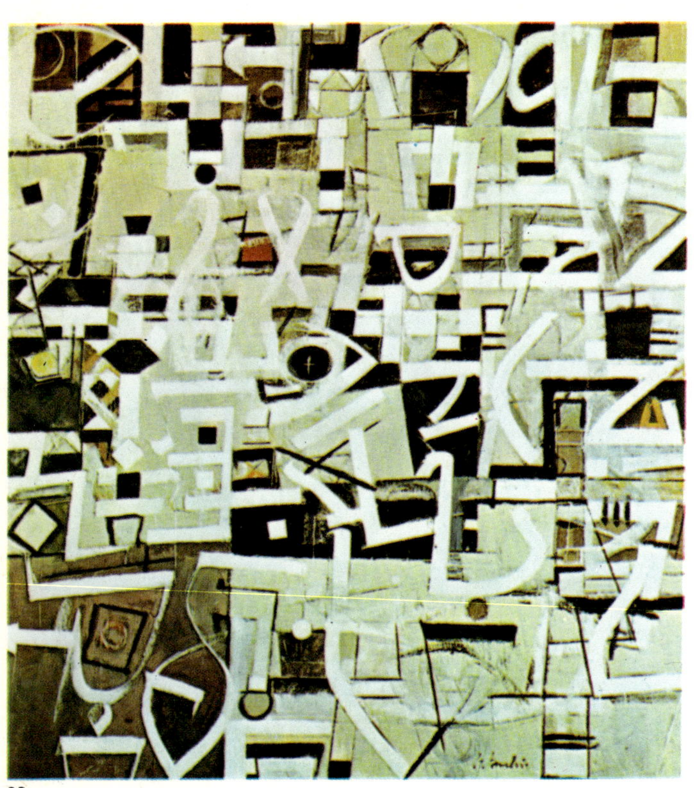

39

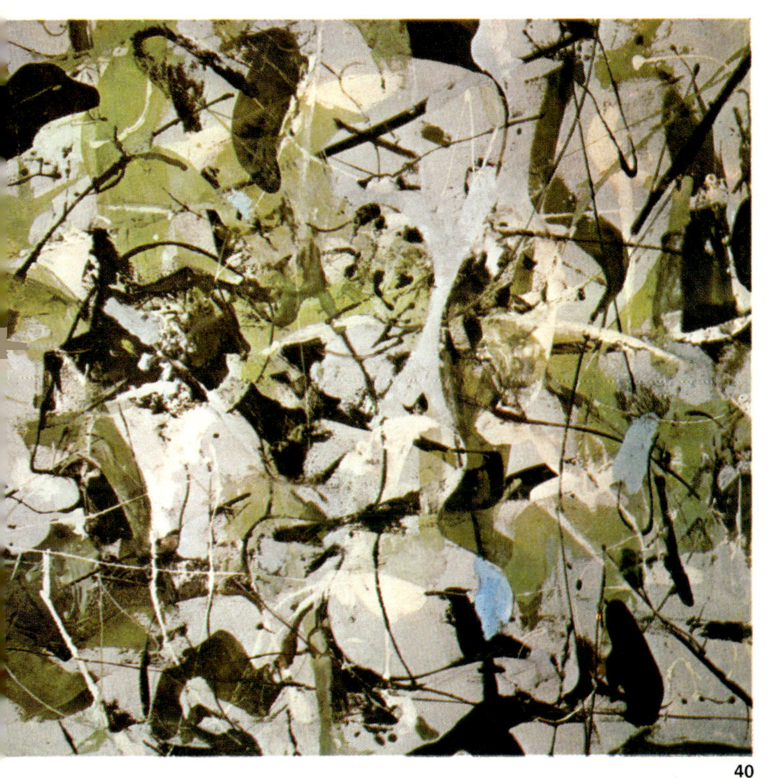

40

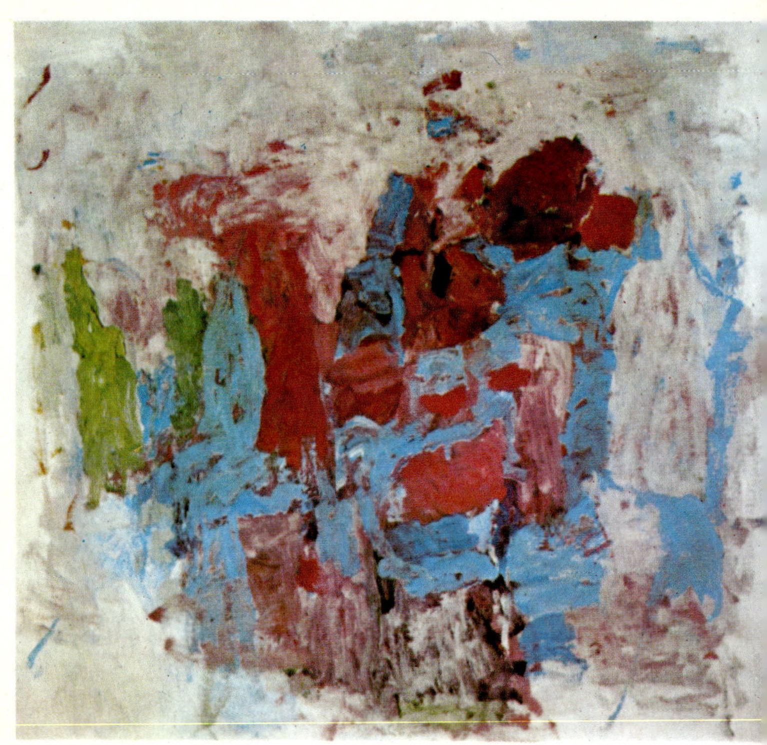

41

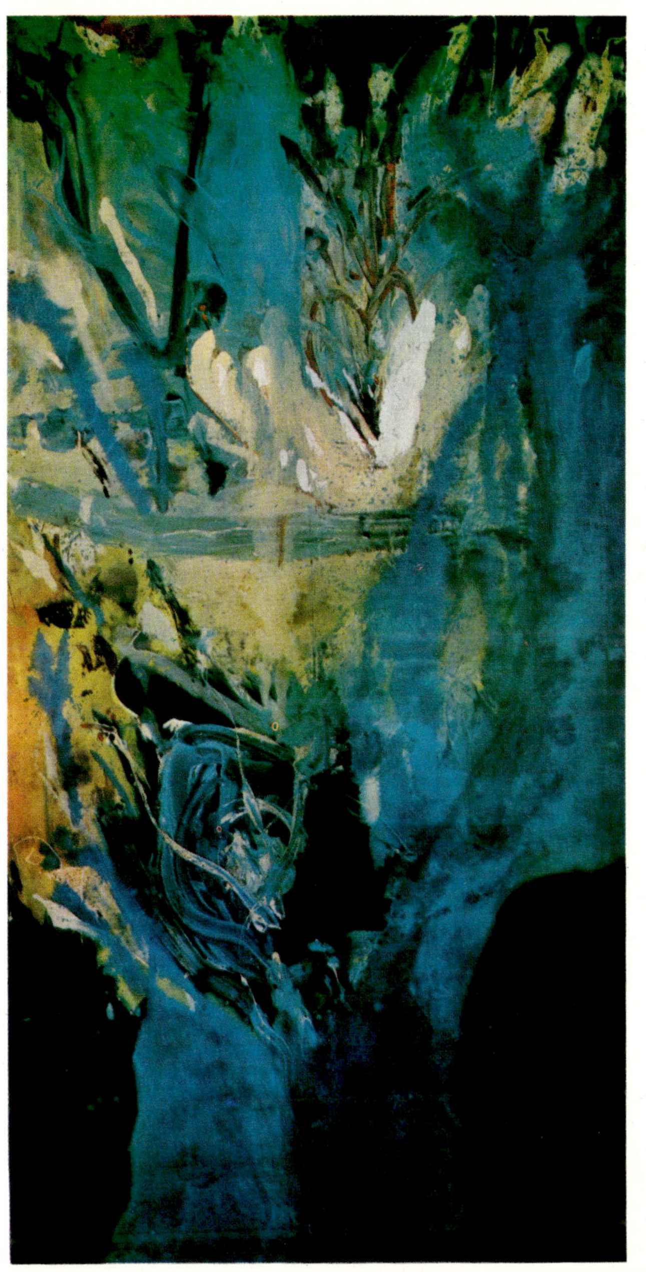

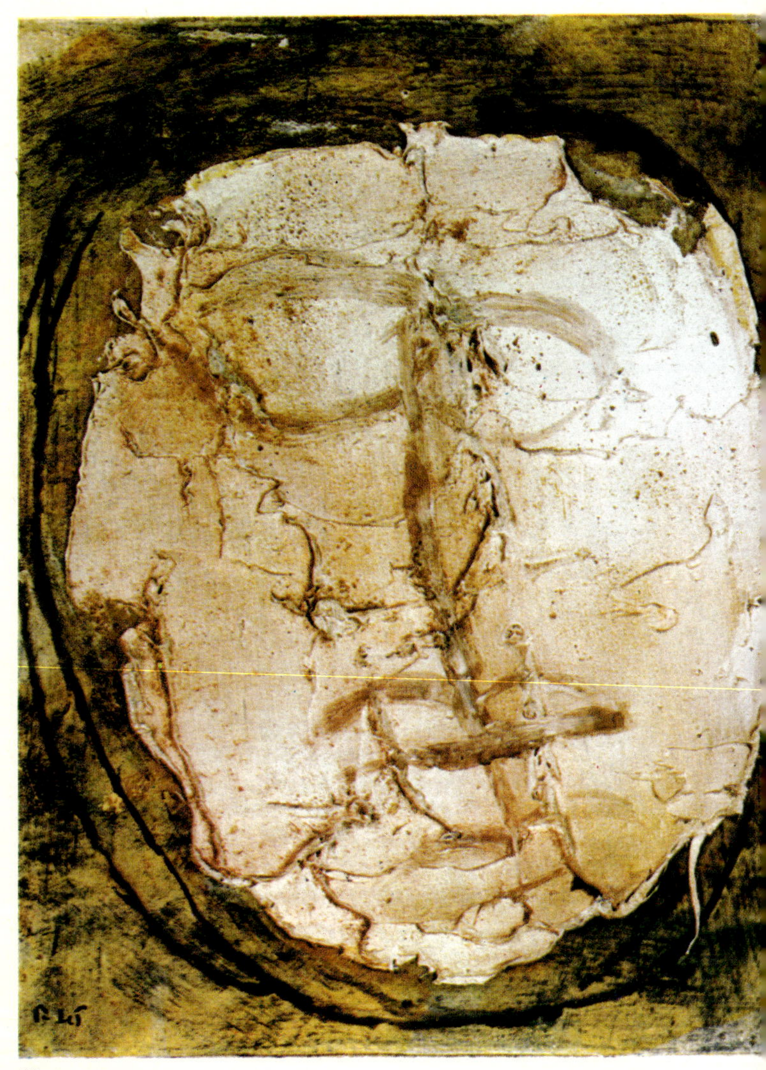

43

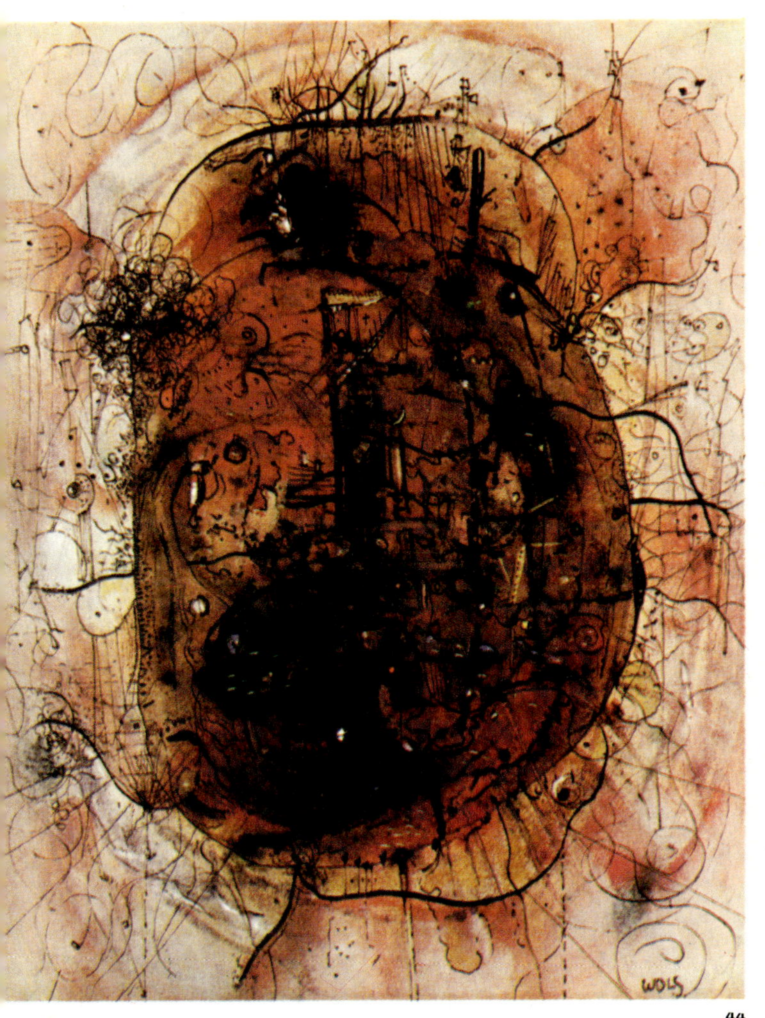

44

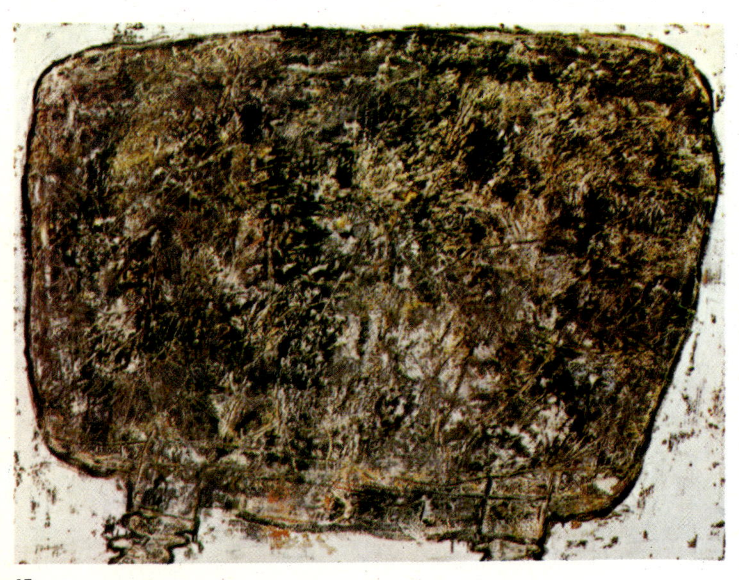

45

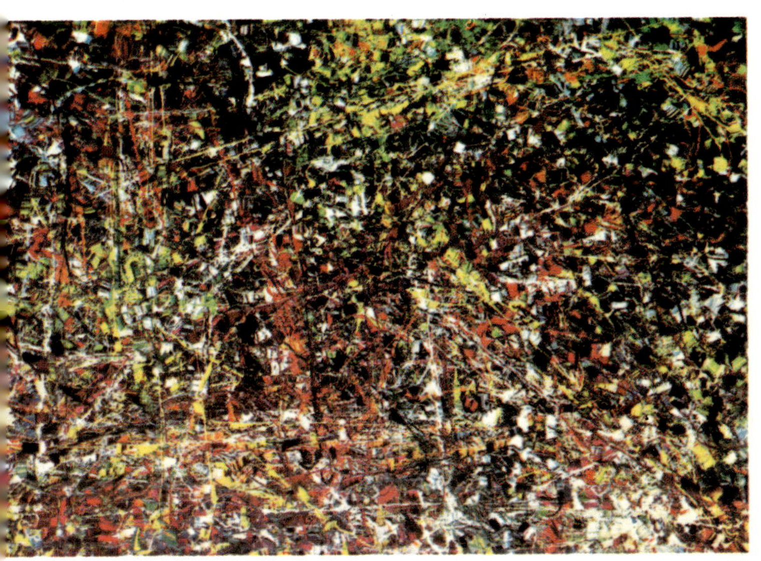

46

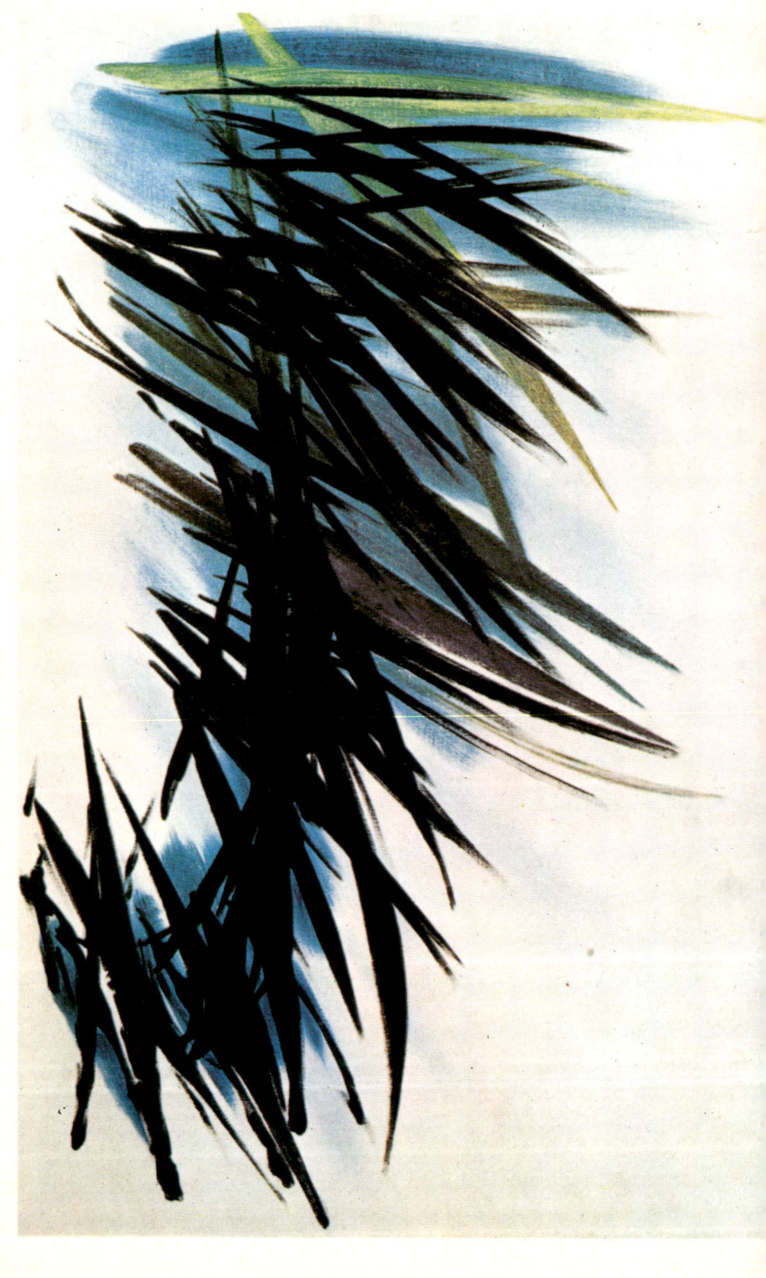

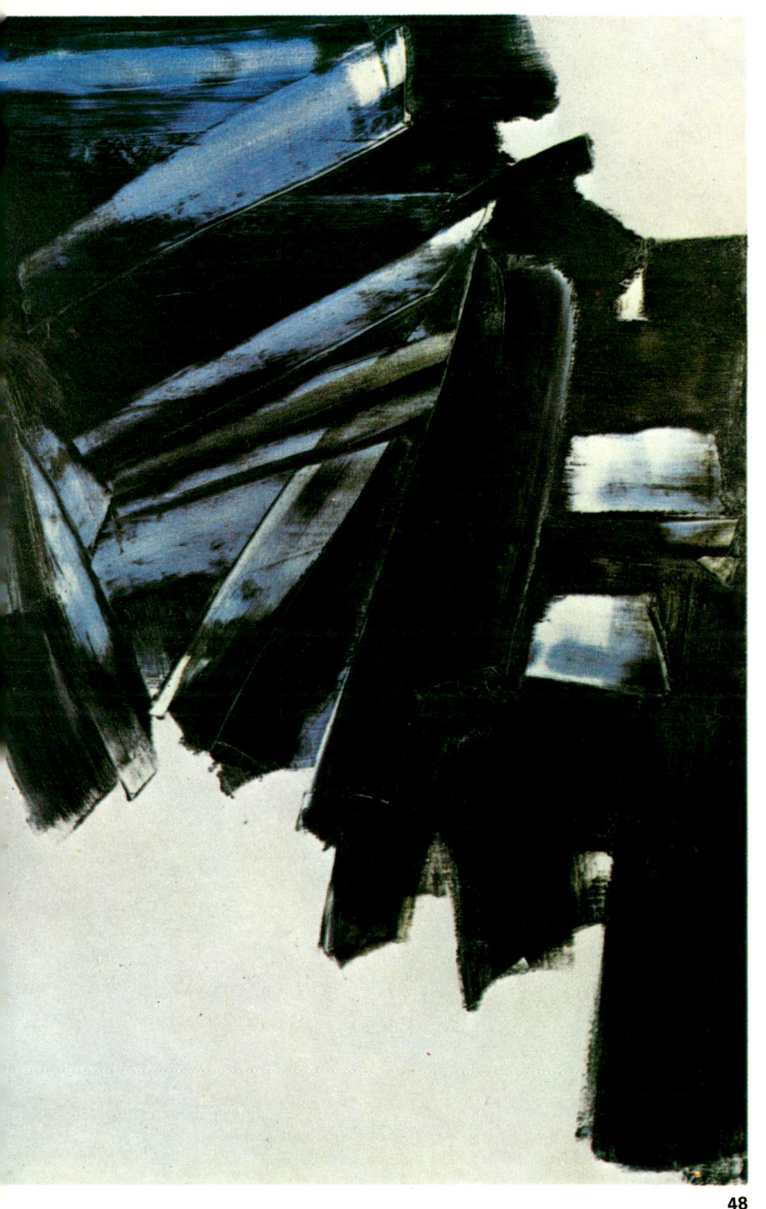

48

47

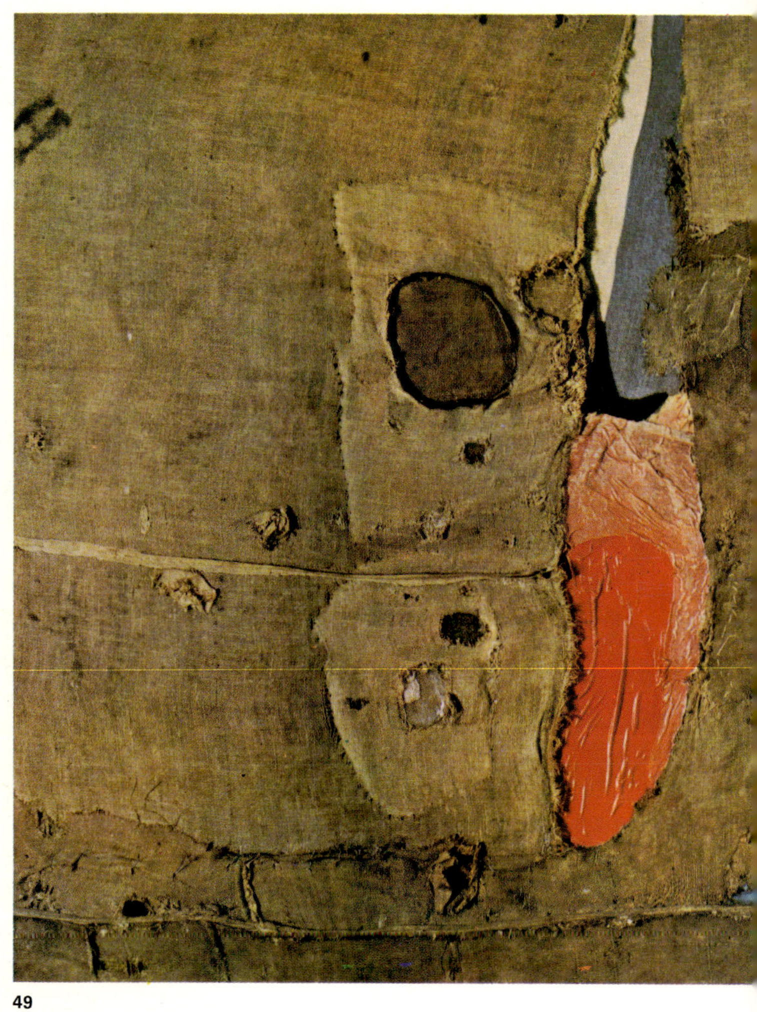

49

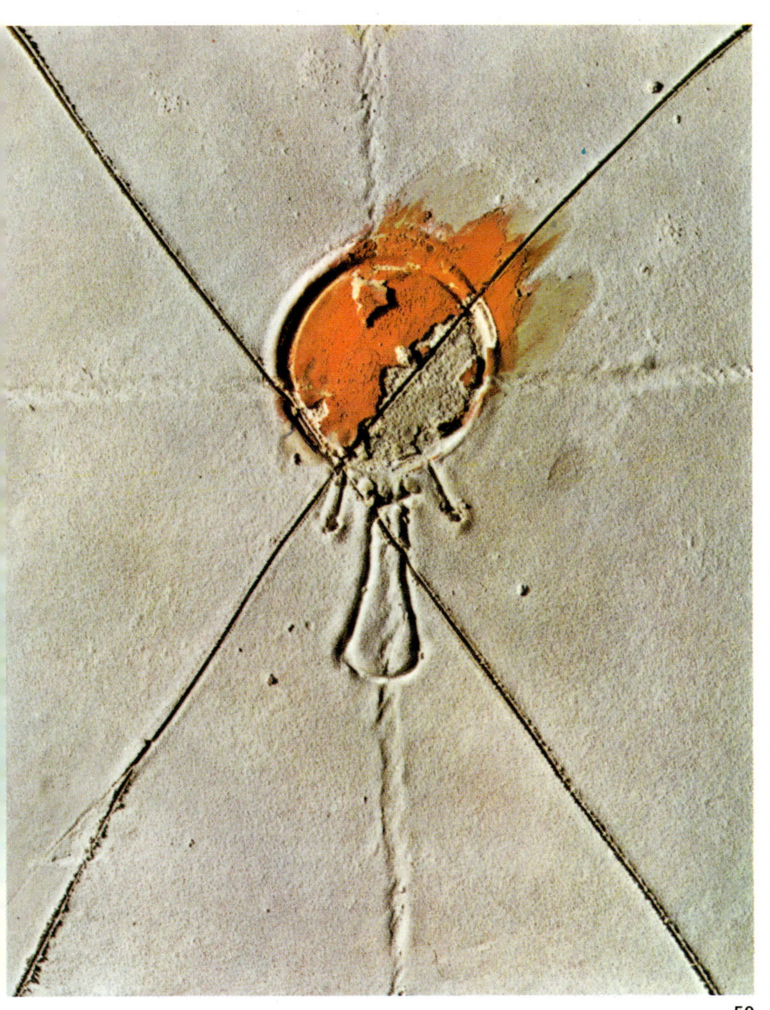

50

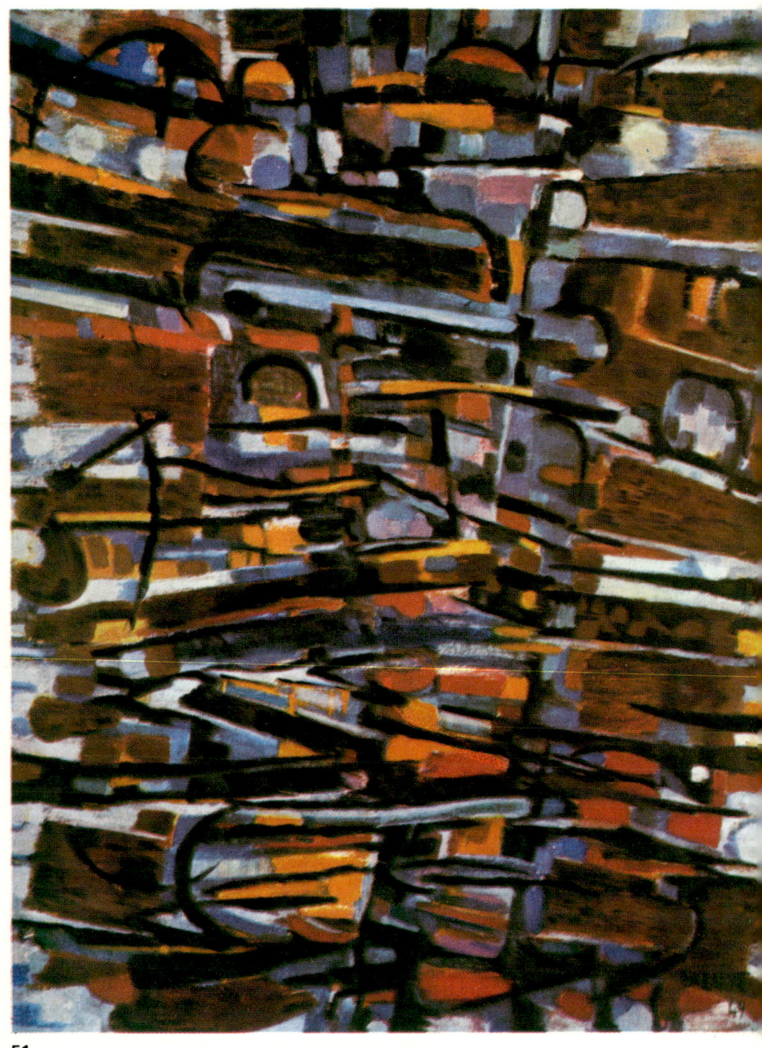

51

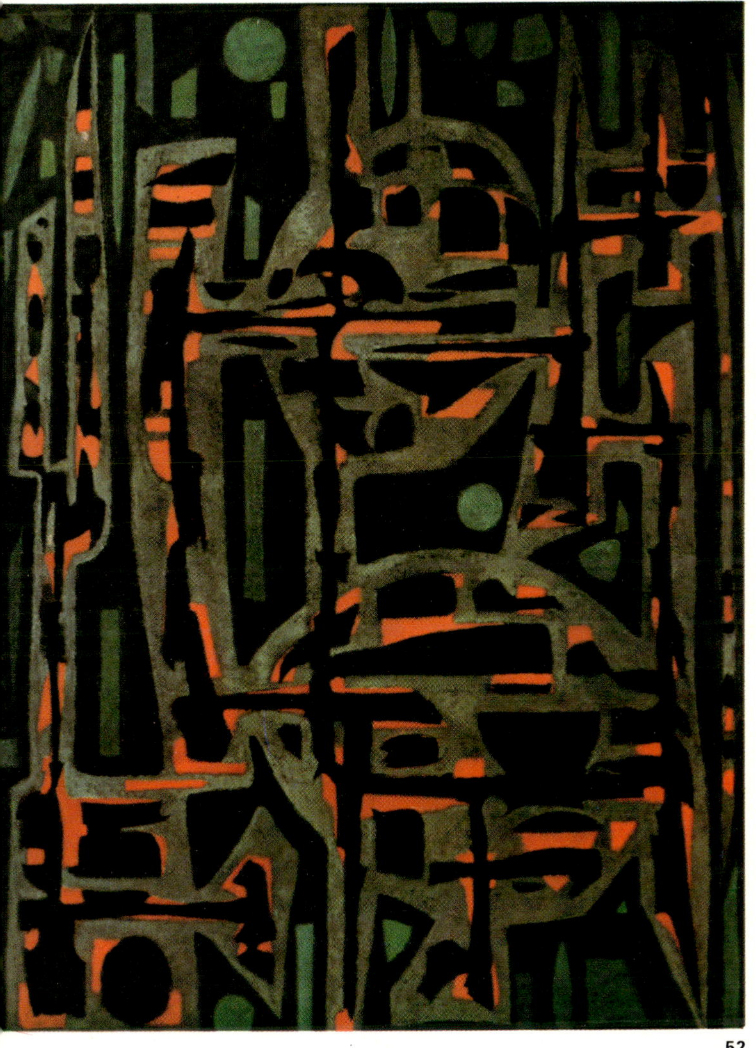

52

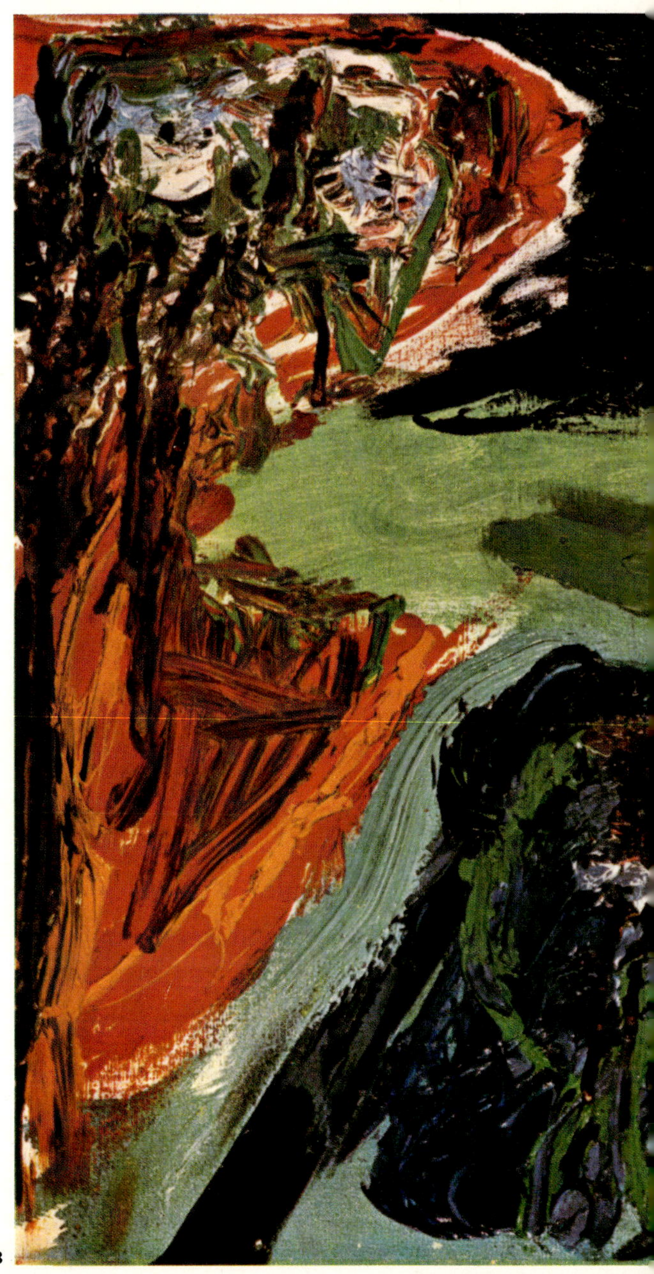

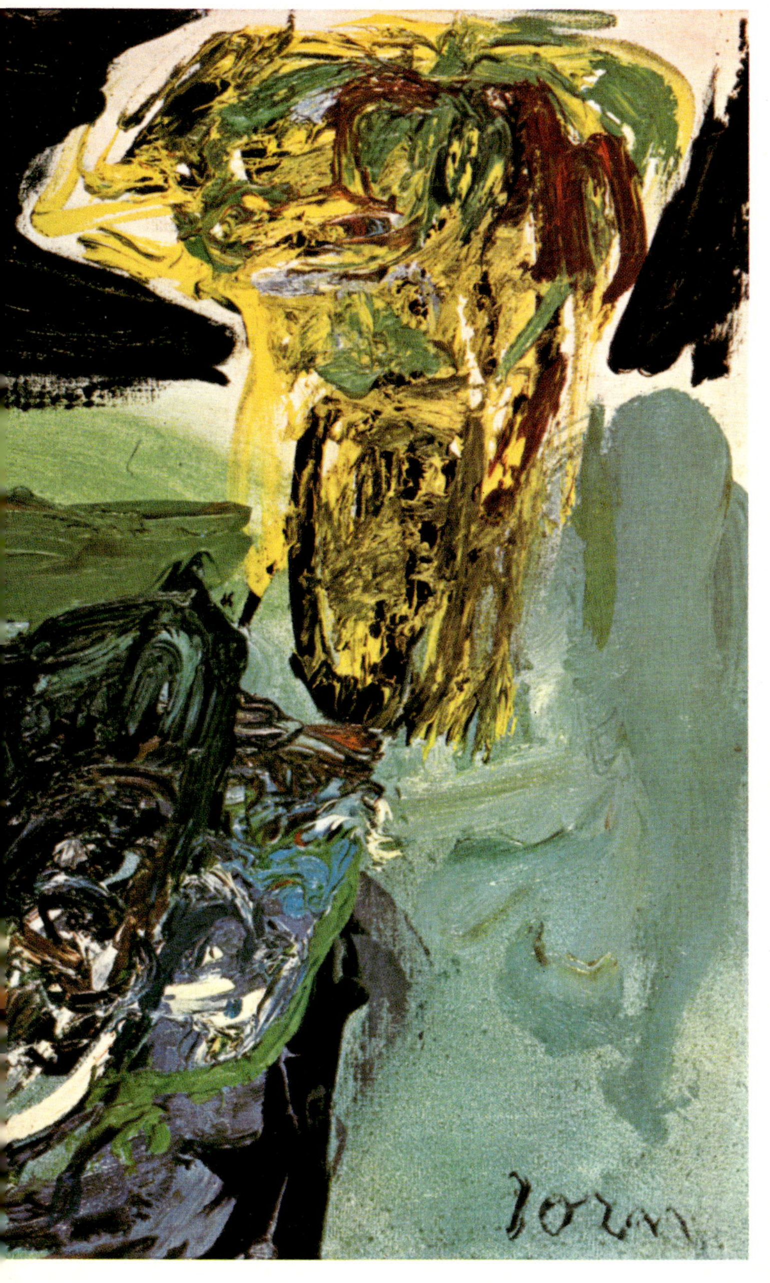
Jorn

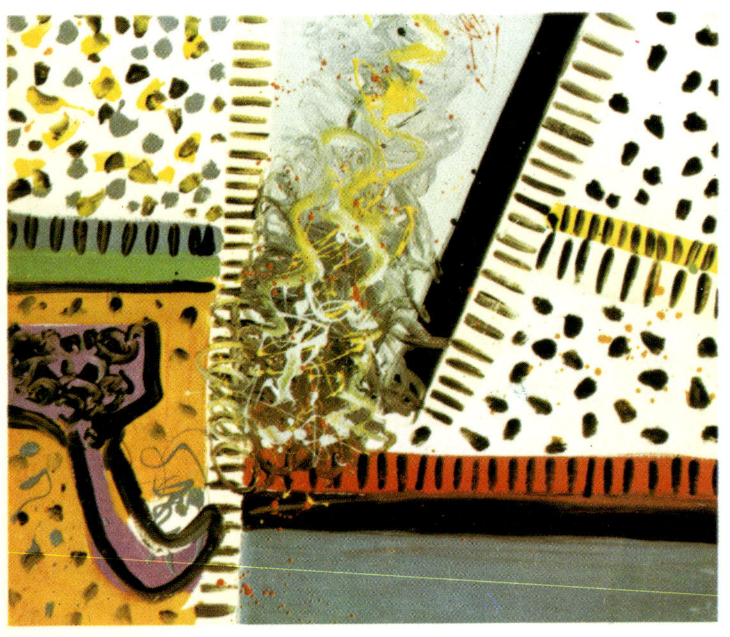

54

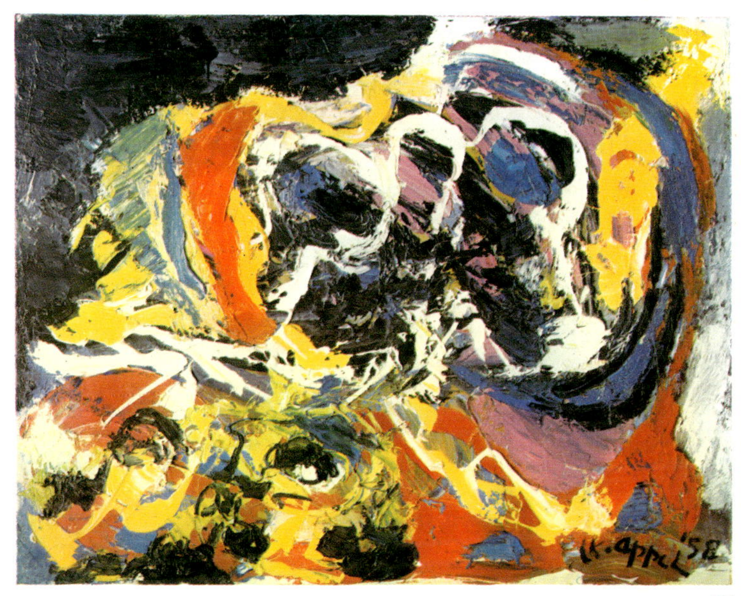

55

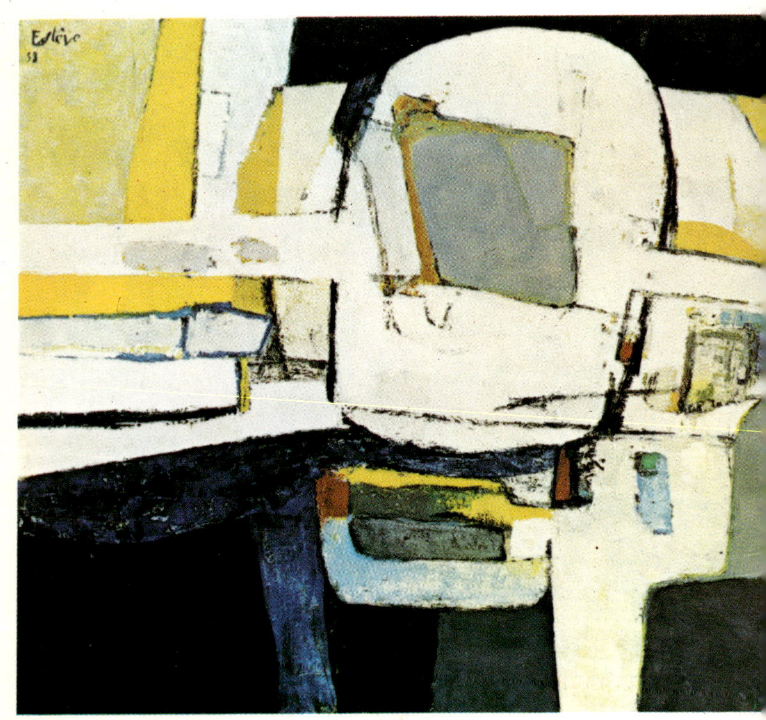

56

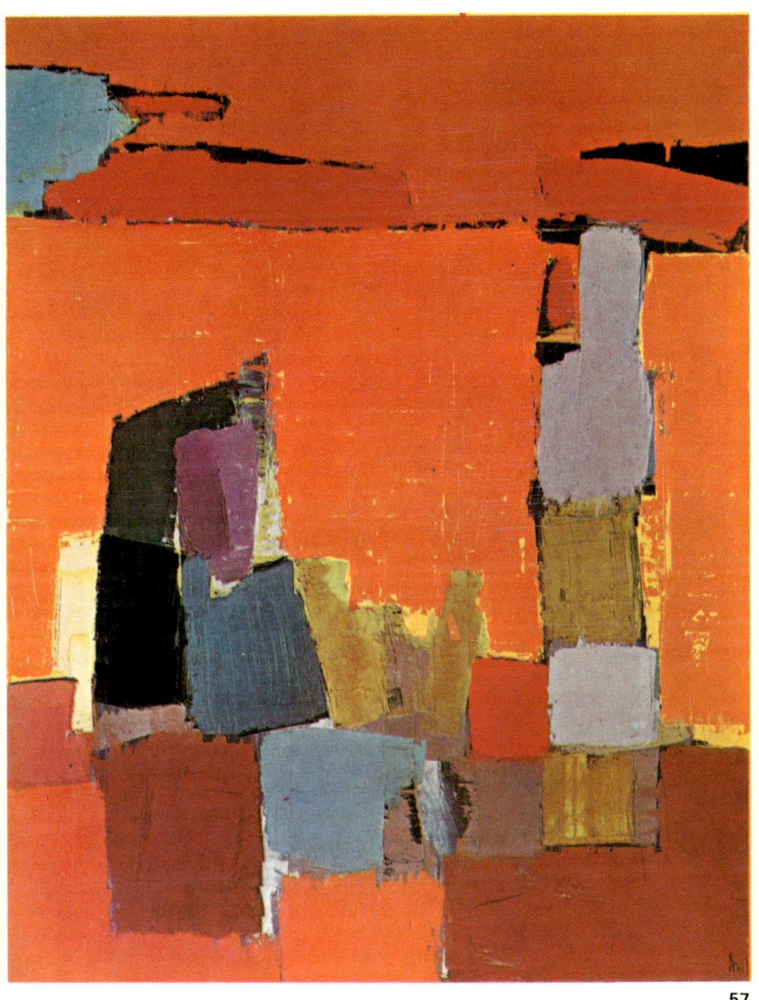

57

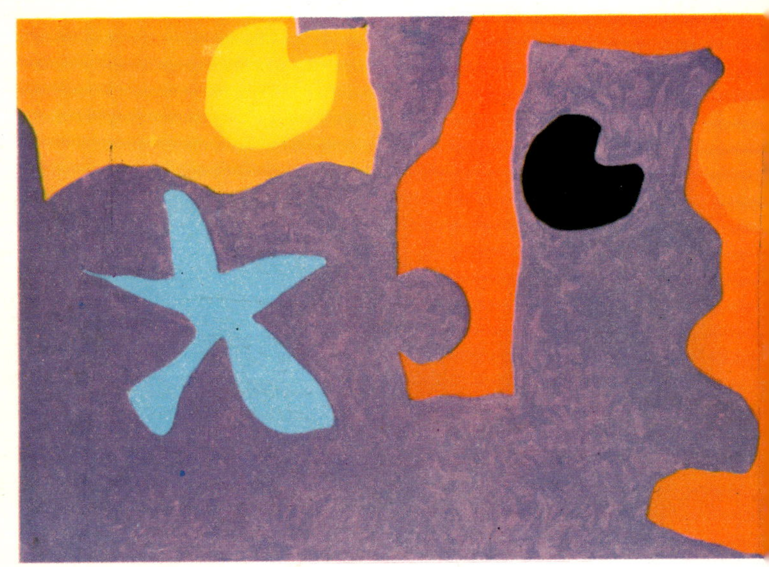

58

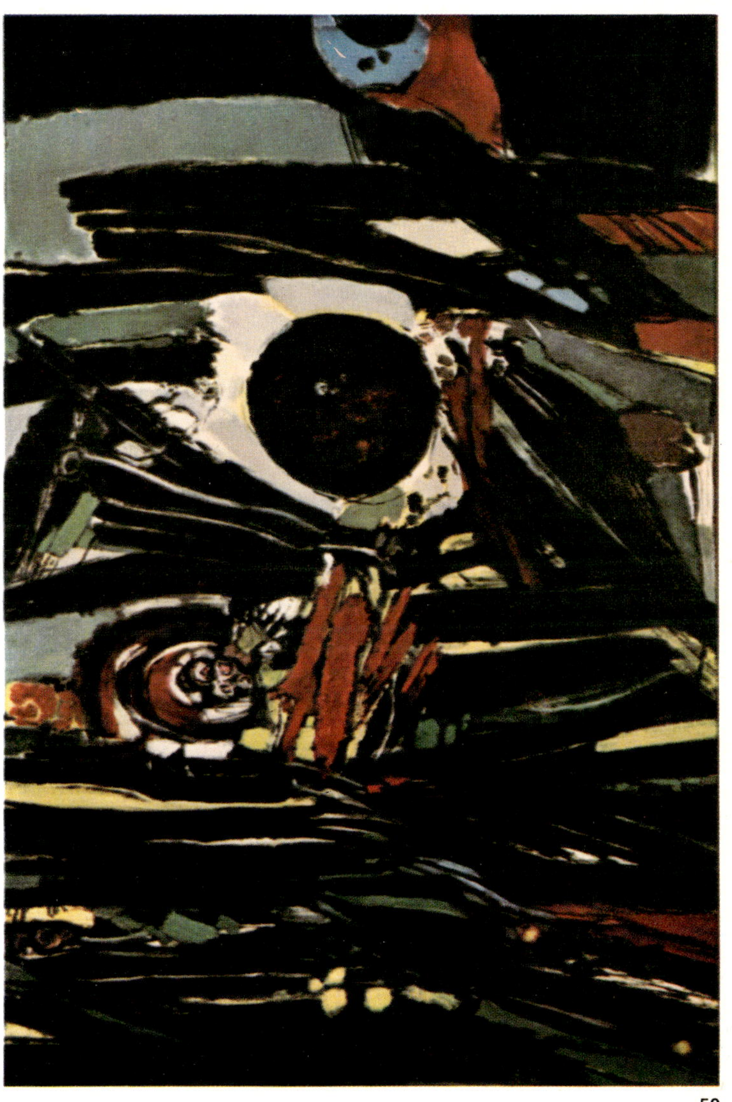

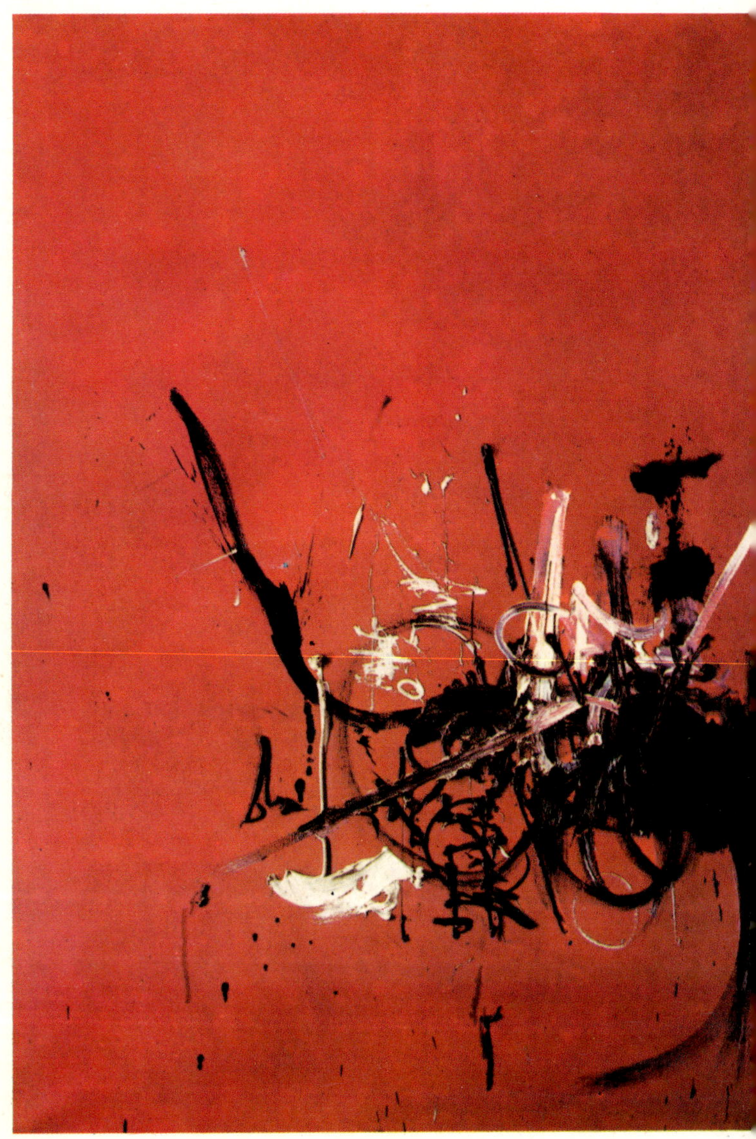